Health, joy, peace, and love are part of your birthright. Learn how to experience them all where it counts most—in your marriage and in your home.

The
SPIRIT
LED
FAMILY

*by Grace Robley and
Wendell (Rob) Robley, M.D.*

Whitaker House
504 LAUREL DRIVE, MONROEVILLE, PA 15146

Cover illustration by Rudy Falsetti

Published by:
Whitaker House
504 Laurel Drive
Monroeville, Pa. 15146

Scripture quoted from The Amplified Bible:
The Amplified Old Testament © 1962, 1964 by Zonder-
van Publishing House
The Amplified New Testament © 1954, 1958 The Lock-
man Foundation
Used by permission.

DEDICATION

This book is dedicated to our family—both blood and spiritual—who brought these teachings into being through their personal problems and daily needs.

Contents

Foreword

At some time in every Christian's life, he will be exposed to teaching that will set him free. Often the instruction is rejected as too far-out or too simple to meet human need.

The concepts set forth in this book by Rob and Grace Robley are not revolutionary. They have existed since God revealed Himself to man.

You will find as you read, allowing the Holy Spirit to minister to you through the Robleys' teaching, that the reality of complete obedience to God and the leadership of Jesus in your life are mandatory.

God is, indeed, still on His throne and through His son Jesus Christ and His Holy Spirit, He is ready and willing to guide your life, if you call on Him for direction.

Rob and Grace, through much prayer and searching, have written a teaching manual to help families build their lives on the solid foundation of Christ's words.

I am grateful they have taken my family into their hearts and their home. They have shown us, by their example, how Jesus has led them all the way amidst the day-to-day problems that exist in all our lives.

The questions they have posed for you will help you search out your lives and your relationships. I hope you, like me, will find yourself with eyes and ears now open instead of closed.

Pray with sincere hearts the prayers Rob and Grace have given you to pray. Search your lives with the questions they have presented for your consideration. And accept the Holy Spirit's guidance to make this book's teaching real to you, as He has made it real to me.

You will discover *The Spirit Led Family* to be a beautiful, maturing-in-the-Lord experience.

Michael Esses

Introduction

We are not playing games: these principles work! In daily life, Christianity is practical. We have found the principles presented throughout these pages to be very effective in our own lives and in the lives of others. But nothing will work for you, unless you are willing to look at your life, commit yourself to God, and allow Him to burn out the trash.

We believe God's Word is true. He intends to present us before Him blameless (Jude 24) in body, soul, and spirit. As a way into this wholeness, we have prepared these Spirit-inspired lessons. It is important to point out here that this teaching book is directed to born-again, baptized-in-the-Holy-Spirit people. When we belong to God, everything the Lord Jesus Christ accomplished on the cross can be applied to our lives by the energizing power of the Holy Spirit. The death and resurrection of Jesus Christ opened the door to the Father and His redemptive love.

We can know Jesus as Deliverer.

We can know Him as Healer.

We can know Him as Restorer.

We minister to many of the Lord's people from all denominations who come to our home for study and teaching. Because we teach as a husband-wife team, we have separated our individual viewpoints on each of the four subjects discussed in this manual.

In our teaching groups, we examine together how to live the Christ-centered life in the family. The life-changing principles in this book grew out of our students' needs and desires to walk in the Spirit.

It is our desire that the material in this book be used by small or large groups, or even by a single family unit. We encourage you, as students, to read together the lesson, use the patterns, and pray the prayers included at the close of Chapters 2, 4, 6, and 8.

It is our prayer, too, that families and groups considering these principles together will center their living around Jesus, growing more and more into His likeness and reality.

1

God's Plan for Husband and Wife: Rob's View

Does a wife submit to a husband if he is not rightly related to God?

Many spiritual leaders teach, "Yes, wives should submit to their husbands in everything." According to some of these leaders, "everything" includes accompanying your husband to bars or discotheques and "doing whatever he says," no matter how unscriptural it is.

The principle

Our submission to each other is based on our submission to God. Ephesians 5:21 points out that we are to submit ourselves to one another in the fear of God. That phrase "in the fear of God" means that our submission to each other is related to our primary allegiance to God. We obey Him first.

15

Obedience to God is first

God is primarily interested in personal relationships with His people. He wants father/son, father/daughter relationships, and He only gets them when we totally submit ourselves to Him, living to please and obey Him.

He does not want to dominate us: He wants fellowship.

As we grow in the Spirit, we find we receive more and more of God, and come closer to Him. We find, too, that to live in continual communion with the Lord, we must keep His commandments.

A deep knowledge of God depends upon our obedience to Him. And our first loyalty is to Him and only to Him.

Who loves God? John 14:21

The person who has My commands and keeps them is the one who [really] loves Me, and whoever [really] loves Me will be loved by My Father. And I [too] will love him and will show (reveal, manifest) Myself to him—I will let Myself be clearly seen by him and make Myself real to him.

Equality under God

My wife and I believe we are equal under God, and there is no reason for male superiority or female inferiority. Our positions may be separate

16

and unique but we are one in Christ. God the Father, God the Son, and God the Holy Spirit each have a unique place and yet they are one.

The man/wife relationship is like the Father/Son relationship. The Father directed Jesus. The Son was totally obedient to the Father. And yet the Father obeyed the Son on many occasions. Remember when Jesus commanded, "Lazarus, come forth"? And shortly before that, He prayed, "I know You always hear and listen to Me. . ." (John 11:42).

Surprisingly, there are times when God obeys us. Every time a believer prays for someone to be healed, and they are, it is because God followed His followers' requests. And when He confirms what they do in His name with signs and wonders (Acts 4:30), He is authenticating their words and deeds. What believers say, He does. "And I will do—I Myself will grant whatever you may ask in My name" (John 14:13).

So you see, in our husband/wife relationships some of the things we do may be separate and unique, but we are one in the Lord.

One in the Lord: Galatians 3:28

There is [now no distinction], neither Jew nor Greek, there is neither slave nor free, there is not male and female; for you are all one in Christ Jesus.

Be subject one to another: Ephesians 5:21, 22, 25

Be subject to one another out of reverence for Christ, the Messiah, the Anointed One.

Wives, be subject—be submissive and adapt yourselves—to your own husbands as [a service] to the Lord . . .

Husbands, love your wives, as Christ loved the church and gave Himself up for her.

Joint heirs together: 1 Peter 3:7

In the same way you married men should live considerately with [your wives], with an intelligent recognition [of the marriage relation], honoring the woman as [physically] the weaker, but [realizing that you] are joint heirs of the grace (God's unmerited favor) of life, in order that your prayers may not be hindered and cut off.—Otherwise you cannot pray effectively.

As husband and wife, Grace and I have a joint bank account, joint bills, and joint tenancy. We each have equal responsibility in these areas. This is true, too, in the spiritual realm, where we are "joint heirs of the grace of life."

As joint heirs together we are heirs to His promises.

We are jointly related to God, individually related to Him, and both related to each other "in the fear of God."

18

Some definitions

In our understanding of scriptural submission, there are four terms we should explore together.

The first one is *yield*. Yield means to give away, surrender, succumb, give precedence to, relinquish to, or submit. Notice that the word submit parallels "to yield" or "defer to."

Two scriptures confirm this: "but offer and yield yourselves to God as though you have been raised from the dead to (perpetual) life" (Romans 6:13). And, "but yield yourselves to the Lord ..." (2 Chronicles 30:8).

Submit, the second term, means to resign or surrender to the will or authority of someone else. It can also mean to yield resignedly to them.

The third word, *commit*, means to give in trust, consign, pledge, or to bind. "Commit your way to the Lord. Roll and repose [each care of] your load on Him" (Psalm 37:5).

Last of all, the word *subject*—used frequently in Bible translations—means to bring under control, dominion, or subjugation. "All of you be subject one to another" (1 Peter 5:5).

I emphasize here the phrase "one to another." This means a subjection that is not just one-way, but both ways. In a marriage relationship context, it means man to wife, wife to husband.

Always, of course, our priority is to God because we belong to Him (2 Corinthians 6:17).

Our first responsibility is not to our spouse or to any other family member.

Can a husband be his wife's channel to God?

I disagree with this concept which has come out of the teaching "submit to your husband in all things . . . no matter what."

Leaders preaching this say, "A wife brings all her problems to her husband and because he is head of the house, he takes them to God."

I object to this. I do not want to be my wife's channel to God. In fact, I cannot be my wife's channel to God. If a husband believes, does that automatically make his wife a believer? If a husband could be his wife's channel to God, it probably would work that way. Or if a husband does not believe, does that automatically mean that his wife—lacking a channel to God—has no way to salvation? Obviously not. Each person—wife or husband—must accept Jesus on his own, and have his own personal relationship with Him.

If I were my wife's channel to God, as some teach, I could corrupt a lot of her guidance from the Lord, since I am only human. No matter how anointed I am, I still "see through a glass darkly." I still have this treasure in an "earthen vessel." Anything I receive from God would necessarily be weakened or contaminated by my own perceptions by the time I passed it on to Grace. And in some areas, I would have preconceived ideas which she would not, ideas that might interfere with what God wants Grace to do.

Grace has to have a personal relationship with Jesus just as I do, and should therefore go directly to the Lord for her directions.

Have your prayers as a husband ever been hindered and cut off? (Refer back to 1 Peter 3:7.) Mine have. When I am grumpy with Grace, I am not in right standing with God or with her. And my prayers get no further than the ceiling. Should she be submissive to me if my communication with God is cut off? To get an answer, she would have to go to Him with her needs.

If we apply the concept of the wife's being totally submissive and the man's being the head of the house without question, he literally becomes her savior, her way to God. This is idolatry, since she is then looking to this man for her salvation. He doesn't measure up to Christ, of course, so she often tries to remake him into the likeness of God—which is rather rough on him, as well.

If we rigidly adhere to the "wife's channel to God" theory with its strong vertical order—man first, wife second, children last—what happens if one link breaks? The whole structure collapses. If a wife has been looking at her husband as her savior, she will discover her savior is fallible.

My wife has no fear of my fallibility. She knows I am fallible. But it doesn't make her feel insecure, because her faith is in God, and not in me.

Sometimes a husband may have to submit to his wife

If husband and wife are equal under God—each a prophet, priest and king in his own right—they will be able to minister to each other in times of need. In other words, as a husband, there will be problems I can't solve alone. I may need my wife's help. It may even be that I will have to submit to her ministry.

Before a trip to Israel one summer, the Lord prompted me to begin praying every morning at 4:30. This became a very anointed time of power and authority for several months, but the first morning after our return, I did battle on my knees with the kingdom of darkness. The enemy of God sought to hinder my obedience.

Later, when I walked into the dining room for breakfast, Grace could see I was disturbed, and she began to pray for me. Two minutes after she began ministering life to me, I was lifted to victory. Through this experience, God emphasized to me, "You're not going to be the priest of this household alone. You have to have your other priest with you." Now we pray together at 4:30.

Submission involves self-denial

Grace and I were praying together one day when the answer to our problem came to her. Should my pride have prevented God's solution if

I were unwilling for Him to use my wife to speak to me?

I think husbands have to die daily on the cross of Christ for their families and their wives. They have to love their wives "as Christ loved the church and gave himself up for her."

Sometimes Grace and I begin a reasonable discussion. She makes statements that cause me to feel uptight. At the point of my negative emotion I hang myself on the cross, rather than react resentfully towards her. I don't want my natural man to take over. On the cross, my indignation is put to death, and I can communicate harmoniously. Don't let problems build up in the family. Crucify any self that is reacting, and trust God to bring forth what is right in Him.

Resisting the enemy

Wherever satanic influence appears it must be resisted (James 4:7). Jesus withstood the enemy in Peter when Peter suggested He didn't have to die on the cross. What Peter said opposed the will of God. Jesus, recognizing Satan behind the lines as the one calling the signals, spoke directly to him saying, "Get behind Me, Satan!"

There may be times when you and I are not saying the same things God says. We're not confessing His will for us, but mouthing our own doubts, disbeliefs, or fears. My wife may recognize this in me and need to stand firm against the enemy's subtle attack. Should she be submissive to me without question when I am not believing what God says?

I worry sometimes about finances. Last year I formed a new partnership in my business; we had to buy a new building and there was need for thousands of dollars. I had no faith and saw no way for God's plan to be worked out. Grace reminded, "Have you ever been delinquent in money problems?"

"No," I answered.

"Have you ever forfeited a debt?"

"No."

"God," she said, "has always been faithful. He will remain faithful even in this. Satan wants you to think God will forsake you now because it looks humanly impossible."

In this way she built my faith and rejected the enemy's influence.

At times I have done the same for her. One morning Grace was worried. "It seems to me," she said, "I have to know all the truth or I will be criticized for writing this book."

"I need to know everything first," she continued, "and, of course, I don't know everything—"

Then I reminded, "Grace, you know the Lord wants this book to be written. Satan is filling your mind with doubts concerning God's will."

So we prayed together and found the enemy had discovered an open door to attack her through a childhood experience. She was corrected many times as a child without explanation and, "There were times," she said, "when I didn't know how to behave because I wasn't disciplined with understanding." Together we realized how this early experience had put a fear into her of venturing out. The memory has since been healed so she can move freely.

But I reminded her of God's plan and stood firm against the negative suggestion of Satan.

A man's challenge

Men can help their wives grow spiritually. Of course, if a woman uses her husband as a channel to God, her spiritual growth will be minimal.

Husbands should encourage their wives to have all the beauty, fruits, and gifts of the Spirit operating in their lives. If her husband is her only connection with God, how can a wife develop the fullness God has for her?

Grace had three children under five years of age when the Lord spoke to me about her spiritual life. Spiritual development of the wife should not be hampered by small children.

A woman's submission is first to God and then to her family. But if in her obedience to God, He leads her outside the realm of the home, her children will not be neglected.

Our children were never pushed aside. We were a close family. But we didn't have to be together all the time to be close. Their basis of security was our love for each other as husband and wife, and they learned to share us and give us to other people.

Every morning and evening we shared together as a family. Our children expressed themselves freely and we listened. We prayed together. We read the Scriptures. In our obedience to the Lord, there were times when the Holy Spirit even told us when our children had problems and needed our counsel.

Grace counseled a young woman once who wanted to go to Bible school. She had two preteen daughters and thought this responsibility would keep her from furthering her knowledge of God's Word. As they discussed this together, the Lord spoke to Grace, "Tell her that as she is faithful to Me, I will take care of her children."

On the other hand, if God has placed the wife in the home and she knows it, she shouldn't try to escape that ministry.

The pivot point of all decisions is our submission to God. He is first.

But a husband can be used by God to bless his wife spiritually. He can encourage her to take her place in the Body of Christ.

There are God-appointed offices in the church, and I personally do not find they are for men only. Nor are the nine anointed gifts of the Spirit and the nine fruits for men only.

The "greater things" (John 14:12) Jesus' disciples can do also applies to women.

It is my opinion that my wife cannot have the fullness of God's offices, gifts, and graces if she has to go through me to receive them. They come sovereignly from God and are anointed by His Holy Spirit as she submits obediently to Him.

The godly woman: Proverbs 31:10-31

A capable, intelligent and virtuous woman, who is he who can find her? She is far more precious than jewels, and *her value is far above rubies* or *pearls.*

The heart of her husband trusts in her confidently and *relies on and believes in her safely, so that he has no lack of* honest *gain or need of* dishonest *spoil.*

She will comfort, encourage and *do him only good as long as there is life within her.*

She seeks out the *wool and flax and works with willing hands* to develop it.

She is like the merchant ships loaded with foodstuffs, she brings her household's food from a far [country].

She rises while yet it is night and gets spiritual *food for her household and assigns her maids their tasks.*

She considers a new field before she buys or *accepts it—expanding prudently* [and not courting neglect of her present duties by assuming others]. With her savings [of time and strength] she plants fruitful vines in her vineyard.

She girds herself with strength [spiritual, mental and physical fitness for her God-given task] and makes her arms strong and firm.

She tastes and sees that her gain from work [with and for God] is good; her lamp goes not out; but it burns on continually through the night [of trouble, privation or sorrow, warning away fear, doubt and distrust].

She lays her hands to the spindle, and her hands hold the distaff.

She opens her hand to the poor; yes, she reaches out her filled hands to the needy [whether in body, mind or spirit].

She fears not the snow for her family, for all her household are doubly clothed in scarlet.

She makes for herself coverlets, cushions and rugs of tapestry. Her clothing is of linen, pure white and fine, and of purple [such as that of which the clothing of the priests and the hallowed cloths of the temple are made].

Her husband is known in the city's gates, when he sits among the elders of the land.

She makes fine linen garments and leads others to buy them; she delivers to the merchants girdles [or sashes that free one for service].

Strength and dignity are her clothing and her position is strong and secure. She rejoices over the

28

future—the latter day or time to come [knowing that she and her family are in readiness for it]!

She opens her mouth with skillful and godly Wisdom, and in her tongue is the law of kindness—giving counsel and instruction.

She looks well to how things go in her household, and the bread of idleness [gossip, discontent and self-pity] she will not eat.

Her children rise up and call her blessed [happy, fortunate and to be envied]; and her husband boasts of and praises her, saying,

Many daughters have done virtuously, nobly and well [with the strength of character that is steadfast in goodness] but you excel them all.

Charm and grace are deceptive, and beauty is vain [because it is not lasting], but a woman who reverently and worshipfully fears the Lord, she shall be praised!

Give her of the fruit of her hands, and let her own works praise her in the gates of the city!

A godly wife valued above earthly treasures

Grace has been a blessing to my spiritual life. God told me to encourage her to go to spiritual meetings and conferences many years ago. She would return home and summarize and digest what she learned. And I would hear all the basic truths she had received. She taped everything, and together we listened, talked, studied, and prayed. I wasn't able to attend all the meetings she went to, but I learned along with her. We both had an insatiable hunger for the things of God. And He caused us to keep pace with one another and with Him.

God's Plan for Husband and Wife: Grace's View

Rob required me to grow up and mature in a way that would fulfill my potential as the spiritual person he knew God wanted me to be.

Early in our marriage, the Lord showed Rob he was to allow me freedom to grow. Rob explained, "The Lord made it clear to me to release you to Him to do what He wants. I do not want to hamper the move of God in your life."

At that time it was, in Rob's own words, "relatively easy to do this. It didn't cost me anything."

When our children were small I was only gone two or three afternoons a week, and Rob didn't lose much. But as the children grew and finally left home, Rob began to feel the pinch.

He was fussing to the Lord about it one day when I was away teaching at a conference for a week.

"Can't You give her a ministry that won't take

her away for such long periods? Why can't she teach closer to home?" And so he went on complaining ... until God showed him plainly that Rob's desires were not to stand in the way of what He was doing.

God works with us to mature us when we submit to His purpose. God will speak to each of us and teach us what we are to permit the other person to do to mature into the likeness of Jesus.

The principle

As man and wife we belong first to God and then to each other. God's will is our priority. And if we want to do what He has ordained for us, He will see to it His plans are fulfilled in our lives.

Commitment to God a priority

It is impossible to live a fruitful Christian life without complete submission to God. Many people read the Scriptures and try to put Ephesians 5 and 6 into practice, but they cannot do it. They lack commitment to God. Unless believers surrender to Him, no human effort on their part will bring His best in their lives.

Paul's letters were written to Christians in the newly-established churches. He was not writing to nonbelievers, but to believers. Even when a Christian man or woman was married to a nonbeliever, Paul directed his teaching to the Christian, telling him or her how to relate to the spouse. The people

32

he taught were those who had first submitted to Christ. Then they listened to the Lord to learn how submission and love were to be lived out, even with a nonbeliever.

With the Bible we cannot make up rules and then live by them. We must live the Word of God under the direction of the Holy Spirit. And biblical truth is ministered to us as needed.

The Christian walk is not standing on one Scripture and living only there. The Word lives, and every verse is significant.

God's Word probes deep: Hebrews 4:12

For the Word that God speaks is alive and full of power—making it active, operative, energizing and effective; it is sharper than any two-edged sword, penetrating to the dividing line of the breath of life (soul) and [the immortal] spirit, and of joints and marrow [that is, of the deepest parts of our nature] exposing and sifting and analyzing and judging the very thoughts and purposes of the heart.

Answers do not come easily

Rob and I are two individuals under God listening to Him to know when to submit to each other and when to build each other up. This is our working with God for each other.

Rob's attitude towards me is always one of

33

laying down his life for me so I may live and come forth into the place God has for me.

I, too, have done the same for Rob, dying to my own interests in order to encourage him to find fulfillment as a person.

Rob listens patiently to me, knowing that sometimes what I say isn't fully developed. But together we develop it. I'm not afraid to communicate my thoughts to him because he never says, "That's a dumb idea." When I come to him, I don't come with an attitude of "I know it all," either.

We do not always agree. But if we both feel strongly about something being God's will, we hold it before the Lord until it is resolved. We do not move until we agree.

If the Holy Spirit says to me, "Set aside what you feel you have received from Me and do what Rob says," I obey. Sometimes He says that to Rob. The point is: we flow together in the Spirit. We want God's will above our own.

Sometimes our ideas of handling a situation are poles apart. In the rearing of our children, we spent hours on our knees praying for them. Many times direction came without question. Much of the time we had to hammer out our two opinions prayerfully until we could both agree.

Rob didn't want our children to have an allowance. He didn't want to spoil them or have them grow up having too much. I wanted to give them everything and didn't want to deny them anything.

After discussion and prayer, we came to a figure we both accepted. We decided that to give them a large amount would not teach them to budget or use money prudently. Part of learning is having a limited amount and planning how to use it. In the process, our two girls learned to sew their own clothes so they could save money for other things. They also learned to shop wisely.

When Rob and I make a decision together we pray and talk it over. In our discussion we don't put each other down. We are trying to find God's will.

When we finally reach a decision, it's like we both sign our names at the bottom of a piece of paper, agreeing that this is what we are both going to do. Because of this, no idea is Rob's and no idea is mine. It is *our* idea from God. In this way we don't blame each other if the idea doesn't work, and many don't. But even this is God's grace to us because He teaches us through mistakes. We had to learn how to pray together, to relate together, to think together, to love and forgive each other, to come into unity, and to be submitted to God jointly.

A husband can teach his wife

Rob would not allow me to be a "blah wife"—a wife who doesn't do anything unless she receives orders from her husband. He was used of the Lord to bring me into spiritual fullness.

I can stand in front of groups of people today to teach because Rob first encouraged me. But that's today. There was a period of preparation, and Rob was the one who shoved me from my secure little nest.

His first project was teaching me to drive. I did not want to do this because I preferred having him take me everywhere. But that did not alter Rob's determination. Every night after work, we went out in the car, and he gave me a driving lesson.

In those years Rob was a Navy medical doctor, and we were stationed in St. Albans, New York. Unexpectedly, he received a twenty-four-hour notice to go overseas. My driving lessons, I thought, were over.

I was wrong, of course. Before Rob left he told me he expected me to know how to drive when he came home. It took me about two years, but I finally got my driver's license.

Learning to drive many years ago prepared me for the driving I must do for my teaching ministry now.

And I discovered something else, too. If we want to do what God has ordained for us and are obedient to our husbands, He will see to it His plans are fulfilled in every detail.

Obedience to God brings family unity

When God requires Rob or me to minister to others, there is no jealousy between us. Nor are there hurtful feelings of "this is not right" or "God is not fair." We acquired this attitude when we gave up the right to our time with each other.

Wednesday, for many years, has been Rob's day off, and it became our special time together. We spent the afternoons in the park, in a museum, or taking a walk. We've always enjoyed talking together, and our love and fellowship have grown deeper through the years.

One day we received a call from Melodyland School of the Bible in Anaheim, asking us to teach on their faculty. The only time we could do this was Wednesdays. At first, this seemed like we were giving up something precious—our time together. But we found in our obedience to God's will that the time He gave back to us was even more treasured. Teaching together was a great satisfaction and joy for both of us.

Rob was not jealous of what I did and did not limit God's will in my life. Nor was I jealous of him and his spiritual growth. If I had been, I would not have prayed for him to be directed and led by the Lord.

When the Lord guided us to teach the Family Life Series in our San Diego home, it was fine when we ministered to a small group. But when He told us to teach the series to a large class, Rob said he didn't have to because the Lord hadn't given him any lessons.

So I began to pray.

"I know this is not right, Lord," I said. "Family Life cannot be taught by one person. It has to be taught by both of us because that is what You told us. Lord, give Rob some lessons."

If I'd been jealous of Rob and coveted glory for myself, I'd have taught alone. I would not have prayed for him as I did.

One day Rob came home from work and said, "Guess what? The Lord is giving me some lessons."

I silently said, "Thank You, Lord."

The process of growing together in the grace of life and the unity of the Spirit is not an easy one. We learned it as we raised our family through the day-to-day problems; we learned how to die to self and submit to each other as we came to various difficulties.

Parents should agree on child discipline

One of our big conflicts came when our two-year-old son, Don, decided he did not want to obey. We tried several methods but nothing seemed to work.

It was Easter Sunday and Rob and I were in the living room. Don was in the bedroom as a punishment for something he'd done. The disconcerting thing about it was Don didn't care one way or another whether he was in the bedroom or in the living room.

Rob and I sat looking at each other, holding all our psychology books, and all our other literature on child rearing. We were totally nonplussed by a two-year-old who did not conform to the books.

But it was good for us, because we realized we didn't know anything, and that nothing in the natural works apart from God. Only God and His Spirit could give us the answers.

Each of our three children had to be dealt with differently, because they were individuals. When we discovered a way to discipline Don, along came Carol. She was different and required another method. Through these experiences and others, Rob and I began to learn how to yield our wills to the Spirit and listen to what God was telling us to do.

In our family I took the responsibilities as God directed. I did not save up the discipline of the children to the end of the day and then let Rob take care of it. I dealt with it as it happened. It was as much my responsibility to carry out what we determined and agreed upon together as it was his. Rob disciplined when he was home, so it was a unified effort.

We learned early in training our children that we had to come to an agreement, because we had intelligent children. They knew when we were in conflict, and they knew how to use that to advantage. As the Lord dealt with us, we came to the place where there were no disagreements and no holes for the children to break through. Our bulwark was firm, and they learned early that they could not separate us.

Submission to God is the key

One summer we attended about forty-five home meetings. Three nights out of each week we taught, studied, and fellowshipped with friends and seekers after God. We were used to moving in harmony when it was time to go home, but one night Rob said, "Let's go," and I said, "No, not yet."

Rob was upset, and on the way home we decided to pray about the situation. I didn't know how it would be solved. Rob said, "We either go on your guidance or mine when it's time to come home." But when we prayed, the Lord said, "Take two cars."

Rob's first comment was, "What will the neighbors think?"

It did bring a lot of smiles to our friends, who kept up a running commentary on our "two cars" all summer. We heard constantly statements like, "Can't you two get together?"

It was amusing, but we learned that sometimes we have to do different things with God even though we are united as husband and wife. Obedience to God is more important than adhering to the way we are accustomed to doing things. Sometimes traditions have to go.

When God got this message across to us, His purpose was accomplished. We only use one car now.

Of course we've had friction. But problems are God's gifts to a husband and wife. They are opportunities for the couple to grow together and to come to agreement. As Rob and I talk over conflicts and pray them through, it is God's wisdom that solves them. There were many times we thought we were clever to think of the things we did, but now we know it was God. We realize it was He guiding and teaching us His way.

If a couple yields to God and wants only His will, His wisdom will be manifested in their home.

Guidance from God: Psalm 32:8

I, the Lord, will instruct you and teach you in the way you should go; I will counsel you with My eye upon you.

How a home is built and furnished:
Proverbs 24:3,4

Through skillful and godly Wisdom is a house [a life, a home, a family] built, and by understanding it is established [on a sound and good foundation].

And by knowledge shall the chambers [of its

41

every area] be filled with all precious and pleasant riches.

A wife should confirm her husband's work

A wife does not have any right to dictate to her husband what he is to do concerning his life's work. This is between him and God. She can encourage him, discuss pros and cons, and be a sounding board as he talks over what he thinks he wants to do. But his directions come from God.

Rob decided to specialize in radiology. The only place he could go for more schooling was back East. He knew it was better for me to live in California because cold weather bothered my leg. (As a child I had osteomyelitis and my left leg is sensitive to climate changes.) Rob, of course, desired my comfort, and yet I was willing to go wherever God led us. We spent one year in Detroit, Michigan, while Rob studied at Henry Ford Hospital. And another year and a half we lived in St. Albans, New York, where Rob trained at the U.S. Naval Hospital. During that time I never knew discomfort. The Lord sustained me and kept me.

If you have a difficulty that God has ordained, then He will make provision for you. It is not that we do things according to our physical handicaps; we do things because He is requiring it, knowing that He will take care of all the details.

Wives should pray for their husbands at work.

My ministry for Rob includes praying for him while he's at the office. I pray against the predatory female. I pray for him to have the right patients, to make accurate diagnoses, for his patients to be healed.

And I see the hand of God in his practice. Some things He does are supernatural, like the time Rob prayed and asked God's help in locating one patient's problem area. As he prayed silently, God moved the fluoroscope directly to the spot where the problem in the body was.

Helping each other to fulfillment

The home is the smallest unit of the Church and as such should be just as creative. All the gifts and graces of Christ should be in the home. If someone makes a mistake, then the loving correction of God should become manifest. The person who makes the mistake should be accepted and corrected in the love of Christ. He should not be humiliated with, "Boy, you did it again!"

The only way a child can learn the loving discipline of God is when the mother and father themselves yield and accept His correction.

Family unity brings forth healing, love, and health. Our family was rarely sick. I used to think it was because Rob was a medical doctor. But I know now it was God's love. When Rob and I were in a healthy relationship in the spiritual realm, there was health in our family in the physi-

43

cal realm and in every other area. This wholeness came from the Spirit and from our submission to God.

God's law is perfect: Psalm 19:7

The law of the Lord is perfect, restoring the [whole] person....

Growing in grace

Just because a man lays down his life daily for his wife does not mean he does it to the point she walks all over him. We do not use scriptural truth or any other teaching principle to whip our partners into line or to take advantage of someone seeking to be obedient. A husband lays down his life as the Lord directs, but he also corrects her as the Lord indicates.

Because God has loved me through Rob, I can say of my husband, "I notice him, regard him, honor him, prefer him, venerate and esteem him; I defer to him as unto the Lord, I praise him and love him and admire him exceedingly" (Ephesians 5:33).

I know when I am to yield to Rob, and I know when I am to submit only to the Lord. I have learned this as Rob has allowed me to grow in grace and become a joint heir with him of the grace of life.

PRAYER

... to be used at conclusion of studying Chapters 1 and 2.

Father, we thank You for Jesus and we yield to You. We pray, Lord, Your unity of the Spirit in us. Grow us up individually, as priests and kings unto You; and then grow us together as priests and kings in Your household so that our whole household may come forth as the Church with all the beauty, graces, and gifts of the Spirit becoming manifest.

Lord, we thank You that You have taught us how to yield up ourselves that we might have You. We surrender our life together as husband and wife that we might give forth Your will, and manifest Who You are. We give You all the praise and glory in the Name of Jesus. Amen.

3

Charismatic Relationships: Rob's View

If you're in the midst of a prayer meeting in your home and some of the relatives drive up, knock on your door and say, "Hi! We're here to visit," what should you do? If you leave your other guests to entertain unexpected relatives, you are allowing them to pull rank over what you are doing for God.

Many people would consider us quite insulting, antisocial, or inconsiderate to ignore relatives at the door to go on with a prayer meeting or anything else God had given us to do. Do you see what Jesus was facing when He placed loyalty to God over his mother and brothers? Jesus did God's business and He did not let relatives interrupt.

The principle

Family relationships must be under the control

47

of the Holy Spirit. As mentioned earlier, our first submission is to God, not to our spouse, parents, or in-laws.

Young people need freedom to establish their own home

Single adults and married children no longer follow their parents' orders. They need freedom to establish their own home under God's leadership. For this reason, through the power of the Holy Spirit, couples should spiritually, emotionally, and physically break from their in-laws.

Honor your parents: Ephesians 6:1-3

Children, obey your parents in the Lord [as His representatives], for this is just and right.

Honor (esteem and value as precious) your father and your mother; this is the first commandment with a promise;

That all may be well with you and that you may live long on the earth.

This verse is applied to children living at home with their parents.

Leave your parents: Genesis 2:24

Therefore a man shall leave his father and his mother and shall become united and cleave to his wife, and they shall become one flesh.

Husband and wife unity: Matthew 19:4-6

He replied, Have you never read that He Who made them from the beginning made them male and female.

And said, For this reason a man shall leave his father and mother and shall be united firmly (joined inseparably) to his wife, and the two shall become one flesh?

So they are no longer two but one flesh. What therefore God has joined together, let not man put asunder (separate).

Two become one: Ephesians 5:31-33

For this reason a man shall leave his father and his mother and shall be joined to his wife, and the two shall become one flesh.

This mystery is very great, but I speak concerning [the relation of] Christ and the church.

However, let each man of you (without exception) love his wife as [being in a sense] his very own self; and let the wife see that she respects and reverences her husband—that she notices him, regards him, honors him, prefers him, venerates and esteems him; and that she defers to him, praises him, and loves and admires him exceedingly.

Christ our Master: Matthew 23:9-11

And do not call any one [in the church] on

earth father, for you have one Father, Who is in heaven.

And you must not be called masters (leaders), for you have one Master (Leader), the Christ.

He who is greatest among you shall be your servant.

Married children have a new home and a new relationship under God; He is their Master. Parents cannot command allegiance from them.

Parents should not obligate their children

Parents can exert various forms of pressure to maintain control of their son or daughter. For example, under the guise of helpfulness (and I am sure they are generously motivated) some parents lend or give money or other assistance to a young couple. Later, they use what they have done as a weapon to enforce obligation or guilt. This is a kind of manipulation which, though subtle, puts married couples in an uncomfortable predicament.

Can you imagine how difficult it would be for a couple to say no to their parents' requests when they are financially indebted to them?

We know a young couple who were in this situation. When they were married, their in-laws—Spirit-filled believers, by the way—provided them with a furnished apartment. This was unnecessary because the husband had a good job and a substantial bank account. Because of the in-laws' action, the daughter-in-law resented the apartment and told me, "It's not my home. It's my mother-in-law's."

In another incident, a mother, still trying to maneuver her married son, bought and planned his wardrobe. She even arranged a week's vacation for him when she thought he was working too hard. The *coup de grace* was when she took him on a trip and left his wife and their new baby at home!

An obligation of any kind to parents can change a couple's attitude towards the in-laws and towards each other.

Suppose on a holiday the wife wants to spend the time with her parents. But her husband wants to start their own family tradition in their home. The wife has to make a choice now between her husband and her parents. If they owe the in-laws money, or have an obligation to them, then it will be more difficult for her husband to voice his opinion. And it will be easier for the wife to get what she wants.

Children do not owe parents a debt of gratitude

This is another area where parents can dominate. And a lot of mothers and fathers whip their children psychologically with the idea that their children owe them gratitude in order to maintain parental authority.

If I believed I owed my mother something be-

51

cause she reared me, she could call me to help her and I would feel compelled to drop every other responsibility to obey instantly. This is a false sense of obligation, of course, but when I respond in this manner, I am still acting as a son and not as a husband.

You see, having a child is the parents' choice with God. The child did not choose the relationship. Parents are obligated to God to rear, nurture, train, and mature their children. Obligation and debt should not exist between parents and children.

My children owe me nothing. I have a debt to God for the privilege and joy of sharing about twenty years of their lives.

What about honoring parents?

Many parents use the scripture "honor your mother and father" to hold a tight rein on children. But I looked up the word "honor" and it does not involve submission.

Children should highly respect, hold in reverence, worship and treat with sincerity and honesty the Christ that is in their parents. This is God's command.

But respect does not mean parents govern your actions. And holding them in reverence does not presuppose that we must submit to their commands and requests. You can revere the motherhood and fatherhood in your parents without allowing that to come above your worship of God. Anyone we place before God is an idol.

We have to be honest with our parents and tell them what God is leading us to do. They may or may not like what we say, but our first loyalty is to God.

Dedication to family can cause unfaithfulness to Christ

In order to manipulate married children, some parents say, "Christ brings unity and peace." They do not recognize the changed relationship between themselves and their married children. So when friction occurs—and perhaps the most popular cause is "I don't see you often enough!"— Mom and Dad tell children that Christ brings oneness. Interpreted by them, this means family unity. More specifically, they believe they should be able to see their children often.

Scripture contains strong language concerning disobedience to God because of family allegiance, love for family, bondage to tradition, or bondage to family unity.

Our attitude to God: Luke 14:26

If any one come to Me and does not hate his [own] father and mother [that is, in the sense of indifference to or relative disregard for them in comparison with his attitude toward God] and [likewise] his wife and children and brothers and sisters, [yes] and even his own life also, he cannot be My disciple.

Follow the Lord first: Matthew 10:34-38
Do not think that I have come to bring peace upon the earth; I have not come to bring peace but a sword.

For I have come to part asunder a man from his father, and a daughter from her mother, and a newly married wife from her mother-in-law;

And a man's foes will be they of his own household.

He who loves and takes more pleasure in father or mother than in Me is not worthy of Me; and he who loves and takes more pleasure in son or daughter than in Me is not worthy of Me;

And he who does not take up his cross and follow Me [that is, cleave steadfastly to Me, conforming wholly to My example in living and if need be in dying also] is not worthy of Me.

The Bible makes it clear that we must decide for Christ or for family unity and peace.

In-laws should not think for children
I talked recently with a married mother who had been away from home ten years. When she went to visit her parents at Christmas, "It was a miserable experience."

"My parents dominated me and treated me as a

child," she said. "They told me where to go, whom to visit, and how to dress!"

Her brother lent her his car so she could visit friends while she was there. At the airport, as she was ready to board the plane to return home, her father told her in strong, vigorous tones, "You have to pay your brother for the use of the car!"

This was none of his business. But through this family holiday, God showed her that although she was a responsible adult herself, her parents were still thinking and planning for her.

When our son married, we were going to a restaurant to have Sunday dinner with him and his wife. Walking into the restaurant I said to Don, "You'd better get your driver's license renewed."

After I said this, I immediately recognized this was not my concern. I was still trying to think for him, and God showed me this. "Don, forgive me," I said quickly. "It's really none of my business."

Funeral and inheritance problems

Parents sometimes promise to "leave everything" to their children in their will if the children will care for them in their final years. This usually means that when the parents get to a certain time of life, they move in with the children. And when they die, the children count on getting their inheritance.

Many children end up disillusioned with this arrangement when, after caring for mom and dad for ten or fifteen years, the will is read and they are not included.

We know an eighty-five-year-old mother with a small estate. Her children have been caring for her for twenty years. And for the past fifteen years they have been coming to my office with all kinds of medical complaints. There is nothing physically wrong with them, but they are miserable and need a little attention. In the office they get love, and this is an outlet for them.

When the mother of these unhappy children comes in for her checkup, she complains about what her children do or do not do. Then, while the mother is down the hall getting x-rays, the son and daughter voice their bitter resentments. "You can't imagine what it's like living with Mother!" they tell me.

Once when they asked my advice, I suggested putting the mother in a convalescent home. "She'll get professional help," I told them.

"Oh, no!" they both replied. "We are getting her inheritance and we're living for that day."

I saw then that their own greed put them into a bondage they hated but did not really want to escape.

There are other couples locked into this role out of a sense of obligation. They believe the Bible requires it.

The Scriptures give two commands concerning care of parents:

One, we are responsible for them.

Two, we are not responsible for them.

Here are two seemingly opposing instructions. This means we must be obedient to the specific orders we receive from the Holy Spirit.

Children not obligated to provide for parents: 2 Corinthians 12:14

Now for the third time I am ready to come to [visit] you. And I will not burden you [financially], for it is not yours that I want but you; for children are not duty bound to lay up store for their parents, but parents for their children.

Providing for your family: 1 Timothy 5:8

If any one fails to provide for his relatives, and especially for those of his own family, he has disowned the faith [by failing to accompany it with fruits], and is worse than an unbeliever [who performs his obligation in these matters].

Do you see why it is important to be submissive first to God? It is only in knowing Him intimately that we will be able to do what is best for everyone.

I have seen many couples hooked, trapped, and in bondage to burdens created by family heritage, final illness, and death. They were so involved in tradition, they could not receive God's guidance concerning final decisions and funeral arrangements. We should not make judgments based upon the way we have always done things. Decisions should be made through the leadership of the Holy Spirit.

It is God's plan for us to care for the elderly. But to know how to do this we must listen to Him. We cannot be imprisoned by family traditions, desires, or demands. God's will is our primary consideration.

This applies to all phases of the in-law relationship. One time the Holy Spirit may tell us to spend Thanksgiving without the relatives, and the next time He may say yes.

In the same way, God may tell one couple to care for their parents and forbid another to help or support their mother and father.

A good excuse? Luke 9:59-62

And He said to another, Become My disciple, side with My party, and accompany Me! But he replied, Lord, permit me first to go and bury [await the death of] my father.

But Jesus said to him, Allow the dead to bury their own dead; but as for you, go and publish abroad throughout all regions the kingdom of God.

Another also said, I will follow You, Lord, and become Your disciple, and side with Your party; but let me first say goodbye to those at my home.

Jesus said to him, No one who puts his hand to the plow and looks back [to the things behind] is fit for the kingdom of God.

In-laws can put bondages on other in-laws

Our son Don married into a family with a complicated family relationship—aunts, uncles, cousins, nieces, nephews and so on down the line. And every holiday, birthday, and anniversary was celebrated together.

When Don married, he was immediately thrust into their pattern of family functions, too. This extended to Grace and me to the point where we didn't have the right to make any personal choices concerning what we wanted to do.

It was an emotional experience breaking away from this family's custom. If we did not attend a social gathering, they took it personally and believed we did not love them. In their hurt they judged us, saying, "You think you're too socially elite for us." They did not allow us to move with the Lord, or to have a relationship with others.

No matter what people think of us, we must obey God and comply with His instructions.

Married couples can put parents in bondage

Parents are not automatic baby sitters. Sometimes they may say, "Bring the children over; we'd love to have them." Then the next week grandmother has the children without asking. This is unfair.

This grandmother will have to be liberated in Jesus through the Holy Spirit so she can pray about whether she can care for the children or not. She also needs freedom to say, "No, today I cannot watch the children."

Newlyweds do not have a free bank account in their parents, either. If they need money, they should not expect mom and dad to supply their need. Parents can use money to obligate their children, but children can also use it for selfish reasons. Both motives are incorrect.

Choosing children above spouse

What if a man and wife have a firm date to go somewhere together? The arrangements are made. Unexpectedly, the PTA schedules a meeting and Johnny announces, "My teacher says all parents should be there."

The devoted mother will say, "We have to go." But maybe her husband would rather not break their date. Will the mother choose her husband or her son? If they do not pray and find the mind of Christ, a conflict will be set up between father and son, and mother and father.

Another example of choosing the child first often occurs when the new baby arrives. When the little one cries, the mother runs, leaving her husband feeling isolated and rejected. This continual choosing of the child often triggers a separation between a loving husband and his wife. He may begin finding interests and activities outside the home.

Fortunately, some young mothers detect what is happening by the help of the Holy Spirit. And the couple resolve the situation together. The husband realizes he is not forsaken for the care of the baby and is assured he is first (after God) in the wife's affections.

We found that one of our babies had to have a two-hour crying period every night. During that time, Grace and I walked up and down the sidewalk in front of our house until it was over. This was not easy to do, but time confirmed the wisdom of our determination.

What would have happened if we had not faced this together? Suppose Grace had to be with our child during his crying sessions? That would have taken from us the unity we had when we walked together.

Handling the relatives

When I returned from overseas, I received an urgent phone call telling me that my dad was seriously ill. (I discovered later that he used illness to get attention.) I immediately got on a train and rode all night to be with him in the hospital.

61

While I was there, my son Don became sick and Grace telephoned. "I need you," she said. "This hospital is unfamiliar to me, and you're a medical man and can help."

I hesitated at first because I was getting involved with the other doctors in the hospital taking care of my dad. "Your father has nurses and doctors there with him all the time," Grace continued. "But I need you here now."

What would have happened if I'd chosen my dad first, saying, "Woman, submit. Go take care of the baby. I have other things to do?"

But I prayed and began to see where my first responsibility was. It was not at my father's side, but with Grace and Don. It was only through the power of God that I could make the choice for my family.

Circumstances have a way of recurring in our lives, and I encountered this difficulty many times.

When my father passed away (twenty years after that first urgent phone call), my mother immediately moved to try to put me in his place. Gradually, I began to take the place of the Lord in her life, too. She compelled me to care for her business negotiations, even though she had an attorney. She constantly sought my counsel, wanting me to share every aspect of her life.

She called me daily on the telephone. Many times she had a repair problem. The water heater wouldn't work. Or the plumbing was faulty. No matter what it was, I dashed over to take care of things. This put quite a strain on my relationship with Grace, who in the process was playing second fiddle to my mother.

Finally, one day, I literally chose between Grace and my mother. And when I chose my wife, my mother (at first) felt rejected and lonely. Actually, what we did was shove her back on the Lord, and through it, she developed other friendships and grew in spiritual maturity.

She has since released us and wants only what Christ wants in her life and in ours. Cutting the umbilical cord frees both persons.

A family interruption: Matthew 12:46-50

Jesus was still speaking to the people when behold, His mother and brother stood outside, seeking to speak to Him.

Some one said to Him, Listen! Your mother and Your brothers are standing outside, seeking to speak to You.

But He replied to the man who told Him, Who is My mother, and who are My brothers?

And stretching out His hand toward [not only the twelve disciples but all] His adherents, He said, Here are My mother and My brothers.

For whoever does the will of My Father in heaven is My brother and sister and mother!

The impartial high priest: Deuteronomy 33:9

[Aaron], who said of his father and mother, I do not regard them, nor did he acknowledge his brothers, or openly recognize his own children. For the priests observed Your word and kept Your covenant [as to their limitations]. *

Freedom to say no

Let's suppose a man and wife have arranged for their children to be cared for so they can spend the afternoon together. About the time they plan to leave, mom and dad drive up to visit.

At this point, many couples reason, "We can't disappoint our folks. We'll have to stay home." If they do, they're not heeding God. He anointed the day for them to be together. If they stay home because they don't want to hurt their parents, they'll disobey God.

If this couple were free from family bondage, they would obey God and tell their folks, "Sorry, Mom and Dad. We have other plans today. But we'll make a date and meet you another time."

Whether parents accept this or not is another thing. Let's hope there is a mutual acceptance of moving with the Lord.

---

* The law requires the high priest to act impartially when one of his immediate family dies. He is to act as though the departed were no kin to him (Leviticus 21:10-12). This sheds light on Christ's attitude toward His mother and brothers in Matthew 12:46-50. Cp. Hebrews 8:1-6; 3:1-3.

There were occasions when my mother insisted I do what she wanted. I had to stand firm and resist her in order to be faithful to God. One day she phoned to tell me an aunt was coming to the birthday dinner we were having for one of our children. I quickly prayed and the Lord told me, "No, she can't come." So I told my mother no. I denied her, to obey God.

In every in-law, family relationship we have to be like Jesus. We must be about God's business and stand with Him against others who are trying to make us do something He is not ordaining.

Every married couple must be set free of bondages and hang-ups with relatives and children. They must refute anyone who tries to steal the time and activities God gives them to do, whether it is social, intellectual, or spiritual.

Learn to release children when they are young

It was easy for Grace and me to release our married children to God and to His will. We started doing that as they grew up.

The first time we released them was when they were very young. Our house had stairs and we contemplated putting a barricade at the top. We didn't want them to fall down. And being a doctor I knew all the risks of stairway injuries. I saw the results daily in my office.

When we prayed about it, the Lord showed me in the Spirit that we would be kidding ourselves

65

by erecting the barricade. The first time we forgot to close it, the children would be down the stairs head first.

The Lord impressed on us that we had to free our children even at the risk of their falling and hurting themselves. They had to learn how to handle steps as they ventured out. This did not mean we were careless. We instructed and trained them as they learned how to use stairs.

When Don was three years old, I had to relinquish him again. The incident occurred one Christmas. The church committee planning the program asked for volunteers, so I volunteered Don. I didn't ask him if he wanted to perform. I didn't pray about it, either. When I did, the Lord told me that Don was not to be in the Christmas program. In retrospect, it probably didn't matter one way or another to Don, but God was dealing with me.

We gave our children responsibilities but we also gave them room to make their own decisions. We gave them doctrinal foundations and encouraged them in personal Bible study and prayer. But how God unfolded this in their lives, we left to them. We did not require them to pray and study with us if they had another time of prayer and study. We allowed God to develop their spiritual life. Our responsibility was to make sure whether they were praying and studying, not when.

We showed our children consideration, praying that some day they would be thoughtful of others. If we had a party in our home and expected quite a few guests, we asked them to help. We did not spring it on them the day of the party, expecting them to give up all their plans for that evening without asking them. Sometimes we required their help as a learning experience for them, but we did not insist because we had a need, regardless of their plans.

When our children married, I thought I had given them to the Lord. But what kept me holding onto my daughters was pride. And I found myself putting a standard of performance on the sons-in-law.

They would come to visit with their new baby, for example, and there would be a need to change the diaper. In my mind, I would immediately begin reacting, "Why don't you do it, Ken? You're not helping my daughter take care of this child."

First of all, it was none of my business one way or the other. But I was still protecting my little girl. While thinking these things through, the Lord dealt with me. And He helped me to remain silent at those times.

Another time one son-in-law lost his job and decided to take a week's vacation before looking for another one. I had all kinds of ideas what he should be doing!

I also expected my sons-in-law to perform in

the area of spiritual growth. I didn't think they were maturing fast enough in the Lord.

I had to repent of all these demands, and as I did, the Lord gave me liberty. Now, I can say they are fellow brothers in Christ, because I have completely taken myself out of the role of father and father-in-law.

The spiritual release I'm referring to is positive. Satan's counterfeit is copping out, giving up. But we do not give up with our children. We unfetter them to grow in God. And for whatever responsibility God gives us in this growth, we are thankful.

We watched our children gradually mature until today they direct their homes and families under God's headship. They, too, have learned to release us as parents to God's will and purpose. There is no bondage either way.

4

Charismatic Relationships: Grace's View

How do you spend holidays? Do you always gather at the grandparents'?

What do you do on Sunday? "We always have dinner out on Sunday." Or, "I always have dinner with Mother."

A tradition is anything we always do; it is something we don't even have to pray about any more. We just do it.

"I always wash on Monday and vacuum on Tuesday." Would you hear God if He suggested you change your schedule?

"We always pray at breakfast." What if God asks you to pray some other time during the day?

The principle

Jesus died to free us from traditions—the way we *always* do things, regardless of changing circumstances.

Honoring God: Romans 14:6-9

He who observes the day, observes it in honor of the Lord. He also who eats, eats in honor of the Lord, since he gives thanks to God; while he who abstains, abstains in honor of the Lord and gives thanks to God.

None of us lives to himself (but to the Lord), and none of us dies to himself (but to the Lord, for)

If we live, we live to the Lord, and if we die, we die to the Lord. So then, whether we live or we die, we belong to the Lord.

For Christ died and lived again for this very purpose, that He might be Lord both of the dead and of the living.

Redeemed from tradition: 1 Peter 1:18, 19

You must know (recognize) that you were redeemed (ransomed) from the useless (fruitless) way of living inherited by tradition from [your] forefathers, not with corruptible things [such as] silver and gold.

But [you were purchased] with the precious blood of Christ, the Messiah, like that of a [sacrificial] lamb without blemish or spot.

Breaking family traditions

I used to think I had to make gifts at Christmas so they would have a personal touch. I wanted them to say to the recipient, "I loved you enough to make this for you." Because of my self-imposed task, some Christmases were not exciting for me. I was trying frantically to finish all the gifts.

Another tradition of mine was creating all my own Christmas decorations. The year we moved into the home we built in San Diego, it was on the church's list for a home tour. And they wanted it decorated for Christmas. I was so busy knocking myself out doing this, I did not care if Christmas came or not. It wasn't Christ's birthday, but a hectic day for me.

I complained but didn't consider giving up making gifts and ornaments. I felt compelled to carry out these family traditions. When I prayed about it, the Holy Spirit came in and broke them up, bringing me freedom. Now I pray about giving gifts. Do I make them? Do we exchange gifts? Do we give gifts at all? What kind of gifts do we give? Do I decorate the house?

When I prayed about giving gifts, I was amazed at God's choices for people. They were not what I would have chosen in the past. I used to choose gifts out of my own likes and dislikes. If I bought candy, I bought the kind I liked. When I started listening to the Lord, my pattern of giving changed.

Breaking loose from a traditional Thanksgiving was traumatic for our whole family. When Rob and I were married, we moved away from our parents. In doing so, we established our own

71

family traditions and they became ingrained in us. We learned, sometimes painfully, to give them to the Lord so He could sort them and give back to us what was right.

One Thanksgiving, He had us go to the retirement center to have dinner with Rob's mother. Another Thanksgiving we went to a restaurant for dinner with all the family.

We need to pray things through, and in the Spirit come against anything in us that does not want to break traditions. We are creatures of habit. But habits sometimes battle the Spirit. The Lord will deal with that in us that wants to repeat itself in the old traditional way, if we'll listen to Him. Sometimes traditions include what He has given us by the Spirit in the past. But today He may require something different. We must be free to move in God in all things.

In holiday traditions, Rob and I had to die to the in-laws' traditions of having all the family and grandchildren in our home. God dealt with us so we were not jealous of the children when they went to other in-laws' homes to celebrate a holiday. We did not insist they spend it with us but gave them liberty to be where God wanted them to be.

Another tradition God guided us in concerned the care of Rob's mother. When she came to the place where she could not live in her own apartment, we found we were going to have to find a place for her to live. I was willing for her to live with us and told the Lord I'd wait on her all day and all night if He required it. He gave me freedom in the Spirit to pray this way.

When Rob and I were praying about it, the Lord made it clear she was not to be in our home. And one day He directed me to go down and talk to her.

Chatting with Grammie, the Spirit of God ministered and I discovered she always wanted to go to a retirement center, but didn't want to spend the money. This, she said, would displease her daughter.

Rob agreed to use his part of the inheritance to pay for Grammie to enter the rest home. "I want to pay you back for my education," he told her. "It cost you just about the same amount of money it will cost to go into the convalescent home. You can take it from my inheritance."

This relieved Grammie's thinking.

Then Rob discussed the matter with his sister. She resisted at first because she considered the rest home like an "old poor house." She had not investigated its facilities and was unaware of its modern conveniences and professional help.

Grammie was happy at the retirement center. She did many things for herself, and this kept her active. She also had opportunities to be with others. She attended prayer groups, Bible studies and programs. If she'd been with us, she would not have been so independent or contented. She also found a ministry to help many discouraged, disappointed people there, because she herself had developed a cheerful outlook on life.

Severing natural relationships

Natural relationships are given to us by the Lord, but sometimes they have to be broken so there can be a new relationship in the Lord. We counseled a young couple once and found that the husband had to cut the natural bond between himself and his mother in order to maintain a healthy relationship with his wife.

Mother/daughter, mother/son, father/daughter, father/son ties must be severed so we can relate to each other, not on a natural level, but through the love of Jesus.

Natural mother love may be indiscriminate, too open, too free. Or it may be close, demanding and possessive. If you tend to be a giving person, you will be a giving mother. If you tend to be a taking person, you will be a taking mother. But in the Lord, there is a giving and a taking, and He directs the timing. This kind of relationship with others is free and honest. An individual held by the love of Jesus does not feel rejected or possessed.

We enjoy good fellowship with our married children. If they wish, they are welcome to come and share with us and even ask our advice. But the reason they have liberty to do this is they know they can take it or leave it. Knowing this gives them freedom to come and talk to us. We say what we are getting in the Spirit, but we do not put them under bondage to do it, or condemn them if they don't do it that way. That is their business with God.

You cannot surrender your will to anyone but God

No family member has the right to dominate us. I think if we are under someone's dictatorship it is because we have allowed it. If you have trouble with your mother-in-law because she tries to command you, you have surrendered your will for her to do that.

In counseling, I have noticed that many people are controlled and ruled by others. But part of it is their fault. They have not wanted to pray about making their own decisions. Or sometimes it has been because they indulged in self-pity and complaining.

If we want liberty, the Holy Spirit can release us. But if we are looking to people for money, security, how to live, then He won't help us. Look to Him and only Him.

Even after counseling, some prefer to keep their bondages and traditions so they can continue feeling sorry for themselves and keep grumbling to others. Some couples continue to have wall-to-wall chaos during holidays because they will not stand up and say to their parents, "We are going to do something different this year." They refuse to express their feelings. As a result, their parents will not grow and the couple remains unhappy. They will not take the first step of hurting someone in order to do what is best in the long run.

We know a mother and father who have been hurting for years because they do not think they see their married children often enough. They have an extremely difficult time allowing their adult children to flow with the Spirit. Their constant complaint is, "We never see our kids." Their philosophy, as presented to the children, is, "You come to visit us whenever we want you to come. And we'll just come to your house any time we want."

But the Spirit-filled children will not allow this because they feel there are things they have to do for the Lord. These children are praying for their parents. And they seek God's help in conversing with their parents on the subject. Something their mom and dad cannot realize is that the highest form of love is walking with the Lord Jesus. This should please them, not the fact that they do or do not see their children.

Sometimes we need to deny self in another person in order for them to grow. This denial action carries with it the challenge of prayer and staying obedient to the Lord.

In his office, Rob sees many parents who use illness to get attention. Perhaps their verbal demands were insufficient in manipulating others. When the person is ill, relatives and children flutter around them. And the sickness effects a fear component, putting guilt on family members to get them to do what the sick person wants.

We knew a family who had to go to the grandmother's house every Christmas without fail, because she had a heart condition and "may not be with us next year." No one in the family made a choice where they would spend the holidays. This continued for twenty years.

Problems like this come to Rob and me continually in counseling young couples. We asked one family, "Are you willing to risk letting your mother get ill in order to obey the Lord if you don't spend Christmas with her?" God can keep parents from exercising illness if we pray.

Don't put anyone on a pedestal

We can make gods of family members by giving them a position of authority or dominance over us. God is our supreme ruler.

This does not mean we will not care for one another, or revere one another, or edify one another. It simply means that Jesus Christ is preeminent. No other one is to be worshipped or given first allegiance. All other relationships are ones of caring and loving out of the love of God within. His love will not elevate an individual to a position that he should not occupy.

A woman I counseled had this problem until the Lord revealed to her all the people standing between Him and her because she had them on pedestals. He showed her the reason for this. The people were on pedestals saying (like gods), "You must obey me." And she was driving herself to please them, rather than seeking God's purpose first.

Children can put parents in a position where, in the child's mind, they cannot fail. This makes the mother and father like gods. Somewhere along the line, the children are going to be disillusioned.

Parents can also put children on pedestals. They can believe they are faultless. This attitude does away with discipline, because if the children are perfect in their parents' eyes, they'll never be corrected.

Ministers can be put on pedestals. Their voice of authority can become for some the dominant voice to which they listen. If the Spirit says something different than the pastor, then the person will deny the Spirit.

After receiving the baptism of the Holy Spirit, I found to my dismay I was still obeying my mother's voice. I could hear her speaking to me as though her words were written on my subconscious, and I was not free to do as the Holy Spirit indicated. I automatically obeyed my mother's voice of authority.

The reason for this became apparent after prayer and searching. She was on a pedestal although she'd been dead twelve years. I thought like she did, did things her way, and had her ideals and standards. In obeying the Holy Spirit, this was a hindrance.

When I asked God to change this pattern, the thought came to request Him to erase from my subconscious my mother's concepts of life. I could not sort out what to erase or what not to erase; I trusted the Lord to retain in my mind what was right. And I asked Him to guide me so I could be released to obey Him.

The mother/daughter relationship was not wrong, but I needed freedom to be myself, not an image of my mother's thoughts and ideas.

We may not always please others

One of the most difficult things for me to do as I walked in the Spirit was to learn to please God first. I was used to doing what people wanted. I wanted to be acceptable to the church. I wanted to make my family happy. I wanted my friends to like me. I was truly a people-pleaser, and when I began walking with the Holy Spirit I had to learn to be a Father-pleaser.

I also had to fight a guilt complex if I didn't do

79

what people thought I should. The Lord dealt with this so I was released to obey Him.

Pedestal-building is natural. We like to have people there so we can quote them, and when things don't go all right we can blame them. If we can slough off responsibility for our actions onto others, then we do not rise or fall with our own obedience or disobedience. We won't depend upon God and we'll shirk prayer.

If these problems are ours, we need to look back with the Holy Spirit in our life and see where we have elevated people to rule over us. If we do this, we can ask Him to dethrone these authority figures and put Jesus in that place of sole command. Human leadership must be in proper perspective.

Learning to relate to others

In our homes we are taught how to relate to people. In my home I learned to lie. When my mother didn't want to meet a salesman or anyone else at the door, she would say to me, "Tell them I'm not home." To me I was forced to lie.

Through experiences like this, I discovered how convenient it is to lie. And I learned to lie my way out of any uncomfortable situation.

When I began to mature in the Lord, I determined to tell the truth in love. The only way my relationships with others were healed was through honesty. I used to lie when people called me on the phone and wanted to drop by to visit. "I'm just going out," I'd say, when I really wasn't at all.

One day I took a candid look at myself. I asked the Holy Spirit to come and redeem this area for me. As He did, it was not always convenient to be honest, but it kept my relationships with others transparent and genuine.

Relating to neighbors

Neighbors can be among our biggest problems. We had a ladder and loaned it to one neighbor so many times he finally thought it was his. Rob went over to get it one day and the neighbor said, "Bring it right back." He'd had our ladder so long he forgot it was ours. We were not careful in letting him use our property, and he became the owner of our ladder.

We lived in a beach area when we were first married. And as a young wife, I was blessed with a washing machine. I shared it with a neighbor friend. One day she said to me, "It's not convenient for me to wash when I do. The day you wash is better for me, so I'd like you to wash another day."

She began telling me when I could or could not use my own washing machine. I didn't know how to handle the situation, because I was inclined to do what others wanted.

I began to grind inside. Rob told me, "Why

don't you do something about it? Don't tell me about it. Tell her."

So the next day I did. I told her how her remark sounded and that I would continue to share the washer, but on my terms, not hers. She was apologetic and agreed.

Another problem area with neighbors is "coffee clutches." In some neighborhoods coffee times destroy friendships. Neighbors talk about ladies not present, and when those ladies are there the next day, they talk about someone else.

The Bible says that every idle, inoperative word will be held against us. So much of our conversation is idle. Unless it is directed by the Spirit, it will have no meaning.

In relating to people as a neighbor, I didn't know how to leave a home graciously when it was time to go. Even though I'd said goodnight, it was difficult getting out the door. Rob would ask, "Why are you always the last one to leave, no matter where we go?" Why did I linger and stay after I said I was going? I didn't know. I asked the Lord to help me, and He gave me impetus to leave under His direction.

What to do when others invade the privacy of your home

In our ministry with people, we've had to deal with a problem perhaps peculiar to pastors and others whose lives are occupied constantly with others. We've had to deal with the invasion of the privacy of our home.

We developed by the Spirit a freedom to tell people graciously when we had another priority that didn't involve their presence. Often distant relatives would show up at our door and expect us to provide food and lodging while they toured the San Diego area. Because of our mid-western background, they expected this. Also, Rob's mother would tell all the relatives, "Stop off and visit Rob and Grace when you come to California. They'd love to take care of you."

It was not always easy to stand at the door of our home and tell people the things God said, but He helped us to be truly Spirit-guided doorkeepers.

When Jesus comes into our life, He wants to shatter all our old law and old ways of relating and celebrating. He intends instead to bring us a new way of living and relating to others. But we must permit His Holy Spirit to work this out in our daily walk with God.

PRAYER

... to be used at conclusion of studying Chapters 3 and 4.

Our gracious Heavenly Father, You have developed the family, the smallest unit of the Church. It is ordained by You. And we can see how You move in and out of family relationships, teaching us how to live in the Spirit.

Lord, we know it is Your great wisdom that has placed us in family relationships to teach us how to live and relate to others. Because when we learn here, we know we can move out to other relationships.

Lord, as we lay ourselves on the altar, help us look at the bondages that are within our family life. Show us what we have learned and accepted within our family as we were growing up. We want to be honest and fair with our children as You are honest and fair with us.

Put reality in the fabric of our being and help us put away the sham and pretense that is keeping us from being open and genuine.

Search our hearts, O Lord. Help us see these areas and then cleanse them by Your blood so we can be what You want us to be.

Father, we do not know some of the things we do that are not pleasing You, because they are so natural to us. Even in the spiritual realm, they seem so right. We do not know what actions originating from deep within our heart may be from guilt, duty, or tradition. Help us look within ourselves to see those things hindering Your perfect will in our relationships.

Show us what causes friction. Show us this so we may have Your peace.

Father, we give You all the holidays and all our family gatherings. We trust You to teach us how to break natural traditions and develop Your supernatural plans for our family life.

Heavenly Father, we thank You for Your Word and Your Holy Spirit. We thank You for what You did on the cross. We claim all the victory purchased for us through Jesus' shed blood.

By Your Holy Spirit direct us to do Your will. Help us to be obedient. We give You glory, honor and praise—forevermore. In the name of Jesus. Amen.

5

Charismatic Confrontations: Rob's View

Who will guide me? Who will lead me? Upon the foundation of what life principles will I base my decisions? Will I make choices based on fear of failure, thereby operating under law, soul, and man? Or will I decide on the basis of blind faith if necessary, choosing to live in grace, the Holy Spirit, and God? Will my course in life be determined by what "God hath said" or will I look to man?

The principle

The Holy Spirit must be in total control of our lives. If He is not at the helm, we are going to have friction with Him, with others and within ourselves. If we are in conflict with one another, we are also in sin, because we are not walking in the Spirit.

Chart explanation

Can Spirit-filled Christians disagree? Yes, and they can also refuse to submit to the Lord's guidance in each other. How is this possible?

To aid our understanding of this concept, a simple chart was developed which demonstrates how our spiritual life can oscillate between desirable and undesirable polarities:

Grace	100%	⇄	0	%	Law
Holy Spirit	100%	⇄	0	%	Soul
God	100%	⇄	0	%	Man

As we mature in the Lord, we oscillate back and forth between law and grace, soul and the Holy Spirit, man and God. For example, if I sin and allow Satan to take over, even temporarily, which way am I going? If I let emotion and fear guide me, I am on the side of law. My choice decides which direction I'll go; the more I mature, the more I choose God's side over man's side.

Chart definitions

Law represents the law of the land, our spiritual laws, our rules and regulations within a family; the whole area of limitations and boundaries.

Soul is briefly described as containing the mind, will, and emotions. The Bible speaks of it as self.

88

Our mind includes the intellect, knowledge, the subconscious and conscious mind. Will, of course, is the ability to make a decision and then move into it. Our emotions are what we feel: hate, love, joy, peace, envy and so on.

Man is a general term used to mean a relating individual created by God composed of soul, spirit, and body. We have already mentioned soul, but man's spirit is sometimes described as three things: the place where there is worship and communion with God, the conscience, and intuition. In the human body of man there are five senses, the flesh, and the bones.

Grace, the *Holy Spirit*, and *God* are a total unit opposite law, soul, and man. In other words, if we are totally in God, we are in grace and in the Holy Spirit. If we are totally in the Holy Spirit then we are in grace and in God. But if our soul is in control, the Spirit is not and law operates.

The arrows in the middle of the chart indicate our walk and life in the Spirit, showing how we oscillate back and forth between law and grace, soul and Spirit, God and natural man.

Sin causes conflict

Sin causes a Spirit-filled Christian to move from God, the Holy Spirit, and grace into law, soul, and man. This causes friction.

The sinner practices evil: 1 John 3:8

[But] he who commits sin (who practices evil doing) is of the devil—takes his character from the evil one; for the devil has sinned (has violated the divine law) from the beginning. The reason the Son of God was made manifest (visible) was to undo (destroy, loosen and dissolve) the works the devil [has done].

How God views the sinner's acts: Proverbs 21:4

Haughtiness of eyes and a proud heart, even the tillage of the wicked, or the lamp of joy to them, [whatever it may be] is sin [in the eyes of God].

The source of sin

When we commit sin, it is of Satan. We not only move from the Holy Spirit's territory, but we open the door to Satan's influence. And we can become his instrument.

For example, Grace and I can be talking together, trying to solve a problem, and I get angry or jealous. This sin causes conflict because I am not under the Holy Spirit's guidance. It also opens me up for Satan's attack. In my anger, the Holy Spirit is not controlling what I say or do. I shove Him aside to vent my rage and in doing so, I give the enemy an opportunity to take over.

If we know Christ as personal Savior, He is within us. But is He on the throne of our life? In the areas where He controls, we grow. And in those areas, we have a greater revelation of Who He is. He can only move into the various rooms of our being as we yield up self-interest and allow Him entrance and supreme authority. This is the problem: most of us still possess areas of self interest. We are not completely untainted; we still have adulteration in us—we still have soulish qualities mixed in with spiritual ones.

Judging my brother was an area in my life of spiritual failure. I was disgusted with another Christian for not "getting with it" spiritually. I looked down on him, saw myself as superior, and allowed pride to control me. This is sin and it allows Satan to operate. It also put me at cross purposes with my brother, because I could not relate to him as an equal.

The more I continued in my pride, and did not repent, the greater foothold I gave Satan. I allowed him room to work his purpose. And, of course, he used me to fulfill his plans.

At this point, the Lord disciplined me. I became severely ill and for three weeks I lay in bed, trying to figure out why. During that time of introspection and searching, the Lord ministered to me. *"In judging your brother,"* He said, *"you were criticizing Me for what I was or was not doing in his life."* Then I realized that I should have been mature enough in Christ not to judge anyone, but let God be God in their life.

If I am proud or haughty and allow Satan into my thinking, then my teaching, too, can be adulterated. Or I might "lean unto my own understanding" and use my mind and intellect to teach and not instruct in the Spirit.

To point up our human frailty, a Christian can be 100% in the Spirit one minute and the next minute slide back to zero (see chart). In this condition, he is 100% in man. A husband can be 100% in the Spirit and the wife at zero, and as a result a disagreement may occur.

For example, Peter was anointed by God and spoke God's truth when he recognized Jesus as the Christ, the Son of God. In his declaration (Matthew 16:16) he was on the side of grace, Spirit, and God. But later on, he suggested that perhaps Jesus didn't have to go to the cross (Matthew 16:22). In doing that, he slipped so far into the law and soul area that Jesus addressed the enemy by name, saying "Get behind Me, Satan" (Matthew 16:22). Christ did not submit to Peter's counsel because it was not God's will. In the same way, if an anointed Christian falls into sin, a fellow believer cannot and should not submit to him.

Later, Peter had a similar experience on the Mount of Transfiguration. He was so thrilled to be there that he counseled Jesus, in effect, "Let's stay here and enjoy the Lord."

God gently rebuked Peter by saying, "This is My Son in whom I am well pleased. Listen to Him." Peter in selfishness sinned because he had already forgotten the other disciples down in the valley ministering to the demoniac. He wanted to stay in the heavenlies with Jesus instead of going down into the world to serve. Peter slipped over into law, soul, and man.

Not glorifying God is sin

We need to remain thankful to God, always recognizing Him as God, honoring and worshipping Him in all things.

Sometimes I feel a glow of personal glory when I make a brilliant medical diagnosis. If I continue patting myself on the back and don't give God the glory, I slip into sin. Then anything I say or do in that state will not be of the Spirit. Again, as in the case of judging my brother, I must repent quickly. Otherwise I leave a door open for Satan to enter my life and use me.

If I go home at the end of the day still wrapped up in an aura of self-glory, I will operate under Satan's influence and my own self-will. The Holy Spirit will not be guiding me. In this over-confident attitude, I wouldn't want my wife to question anything I decided or did. So there would be friction in our home, because she wouldn't appreciate my self-righteousness.

Whatever we do without faith is sin

When I am driven by Satan or self to do something, I am sinning. The Holy Spirit is not my guide, therefore I am in conflict with God and operating under the soul and law opposed to God. The absence of conflict, however, doesn't necessarily guarantee that we are walking in the Spirit. A couple can be in agreement in deciding to do something, but if they do not decide under the Spirit's direction, they are in sin, because they are in conflict with God's will for their lives.

Act from faith: Romans 14:23

For whatever does not originate and proceed from faith is sin—that is, whatever is done without a conviction of its approval by God is sinful.

The sin of ommission

We can sin and cause problems by not doing the thing we know we should. When God gives us direction through His Spirit and we knowingly disobey, then we sin.

If God tells Grace to discipline someone in the Body and she disobeys, she sins. In doing this, she opens herself up to Satanic attack and conflict occurs. The person in sin is left uncorrected, and Grace is disobedient. There is no free flow of the Spirit in their relationship.

94

Do what you know is right: James 4:17

So any person who knows what is right to do but does not do it, to him it is sin.

Doubt is sin

Doubting brings conflict, because it keeps the Holy Spirit from moving and bringing His solution. For instance, if I am praying for someone and then begin to doubt God's moving, those doubts in my mind keep that person from receiving God's answer—unless somebody of stronger faith is praying too. When we pray, we must believe.

Guard your heart from depression: Luke 21:34

But take heed to yourselves and be on your guard lest your hearts be overburdened and depressed—weighted down—with the giddiness and headache and nausea of self-indulgence, drunkenness, and worldly worries and cares pertaining to (the business of) this life, and that day come upon you suddenly like a trap or a noose. . . .

Satan has God's permission to discipline lukewarm Christians

Mediocre Christians are "spued out of God's mouth" (Revelation 3:16). This is strong language, but it is Bible. The complacent believer does not practice what God says. For example, what if a father in a family is lackadaisical in disciplining his children? This causes them to stay in disobedience and not in right relationship with God. It also keeps the man and his wife in disunity on the subject of discipline.

Anytime you are mediocre in your spiritual fellowship, Satan can take advantage of you. He might even get a foothold in your life.

Passive believers live in the flesh and do not please God (Romans 8:8).

Don't be a meddler: 1 Peter 4:15

But let none of you suffer as . . . a mischief-maker (a meddler) in the affairs of others—infringing on their rights.

Are you a backseat driver when your wife is at the wheel of the car? That's meddling. Every time Grace helps me drive by telling me when to put on the brakes, when to turn the corner, which direction to go, she is meddling. I sin when I get angry with her. She is meddling and I am angry, so we are in conflict and open for Satan's attack. And he can certainly embellish a minor incident until it becomes a full-blown catastrophe!

Infringing on the rights of others is sin:
Philippians 2:3

Instead, in the true spirit of humility (lowliness of mind) let each regard the others as better than and superior to himself—thinking more highly of one another than you do of yourselves.

96

It is selfish to think of yourself before others. If we are late and someone is standing around waiting for us, we are not being considerate of that person.

During a Bible study in our home, one woman parked her car so no one else could leave until she did. She, of course, was the last person to say goodnight. To add to this, it was also against the fire law to park as she did.

When my freedom infringes on someone else's, I am no longer moving in God's grace. We have to watch our liberty in the Spirit. We should not hurt someone else and infringe on their rights. The freedom we receive from God when we are flowing with Him is not license. It respects others and their rights.

This principle works in our own family. If I commit my time to a worthy spiritual activity, but deprive my family or my wife of a relationship with me, I am infringing on their rights. My children or my wife may be hurt because I chose something else over them and their needs. When God indicates we are to have spiritual activities outside the home, conflicts, hurt, and neglect will not occur. God controls. But a lot of seemingly spiritual performance may not be God's will.

We know a minister with two teen-age boys who tried to escape his parental responsibility through hyperactivity in the spiritual realm. When I talked to him about it, he told me, "But last night I led ten people to the Lord."

One afternoon I saw his boys and in chatting with them, they said, "We're going to take drugs because that way we'll get Dad to visit us if we go to jail. He visits prisoners."

That same evening I related this to the father who had come to one of our teaching seminars. It was coffee break and with the clatter of cups and cheerful conversation buzzing around us, he listened intently. "You're right," he said, "I'm going home right now." And he left before the service concluded. The family life in his home has since radically changed.

Listening to man rather than God is sin

Grace and I had a counseling group one time. They were our friends and we loved each one. After several months of meeting with them and counseling and praying over various personal problems and conflicts, we felt it was time to terminate the fellowship. We told them and were ready to bring it all to a happy close. But they entreated us to continue. In the time we extended the group, we had no power and the Spirit did not operate. We knew the Lord had taken away His anointing. We knew, too, that we should have concluded the gatherings. But we went on with them because the people were our friends, and we desired to make them happy. We were not in God's will, and because we knew it, we were in sin.

Carelessness is sin

One day at my office, I received two emergency calls from two different hospitals. They both wanted me right away. I took it to the Lord, and He gave me peace about where to go. I was in my car driving happily along in God's direction. I was so thankful, I started to praise Him and sing in the Spirit. Suddenly a red light was flashing and a siren sounding. "I wonder who's in trouble," I thought.

I was still singing when I saw the policeman in the rearview mirror. And I realized he was after me. I was going forty-five miles an hour in a twenty-five mile zone. Certainly I was in conflict with the law.

I said, "Lord, why did that happen? Why did I get a ticket when I was talking to You?" And the Lord showed me after some serious searching that I'd been careless. So I had slipped over into the law realm and God's civil law took effect.

Test the prophets

This is another area where we can fall into sin. We lean on someone else's guidance instead of getting a direct word or confirmation from God.

The Scripture commands us to test prophets

and what they say. If we don't, then we sin. We open ourselves up for words from a person's self or from Satan. If we obey these false messages, we are in conflict with God's perfect will for us.

Judge prophecy: 1 Corinthians 14:29

So, let two or three prophets speak—those inspired to preach or teach—while the rest pay attention and *weigh* and *discern what is said.*

False prophets in the world: 1 John 4:1

Beloved, do not put faith in every spirit, but prove (test) the spirits to discover whether they proceed from God; for many false prophets have gone forth into the world.

Fellowship with the Holy Spirit keeps our relationships with others clear of debris. And following His leading and listening to His voice guard us from mediocrity in our actions.

6

Charismatic Confrontations: Grace's View

Yes, we are changed when Christ becomes our Savior. He is no longer on the outside, because we've invited Him to live within us. But that initial experience only changed our direction. We turned from our own way to walk with God. When we are born again we do not instantaneously experience what we legally are in Jesus. We are heirs to all things, but we do not possess in actuality all things. This is because growth is a process: when we plant an oak tree, it is an oak tree in potential, but until it grows it's still a seed in the ground.

The children of Israel were promised the land of Canaan. Legally it was theirs, but because of unbelief and doubt, complaints and grumblings, it took them forty years to arrive at their destination. Would to God we could profit from their experience! And we can, if we say yes every time

He confronts us. It may mean we die to what we want, but obedience conquers ego. And we will grow.

The principle

Half-truths, soul force, and habit patterns can cause conflict between two Spirit-filled Christians.

Half-truths fight the Spirit

In confrontations with others, we often discover the scum of our nature coming to the top. When our youngest daughter, Dianne, was getting married, Rob and I were discussing finances with her. She had earned some money and had a bank account. She also had a money gift from her grandmother.

"You'd better save the money Grammie gave you for college," I suggested. And instead of stopping there, I added, "And the rest of your money you should keep in a separate account, too."

In my mind was the concept she should keep all her money for herself and not share it with her husband. "It's her money," I rationalized.

Of course, I was wrong, and Rob said, "That wouldn't be fair."

"Yes, Mom," said Dianne, "Steve and I should have a joint bank account."

"Well," I defended, "The Holy Spirit is guiding me to say this."

"And the Holy Spirit is guiding me, too," Rob said.

About this time I felt righteously indignant so I spoke compulsively. "Then everything I'm saying is not of God, and I'd better be quiet."

And I was—for three days.

Actually, I was not silent because of pouting. But I knew how quickly the enemy could take advantage of a misunderstanding. And I didn't want to give him an opportunity to use me. My own thinking was confused. So I did not speak for fear it would be of Satan and not of God. By refusing to communicate, however, I was walking on the enemy's territory. But in my desire not to become his mouthpiece, I lost sight of that truth.

"How can we counsel people if you won't talk?" Rob asked me on the third morning.

Quietly I left the room to seek the Lord. "Why did I believe I spoke in the Spirit when I didn't?" I questioned. Then He reminded me. In my subconscious was planted the idea that when a girl marries she should keep all her money for herself, but the man should put his money into the family bank account.

How the Lord gave me the solution is explained more fully in Chapter 8, but I did discover that there was a conflict between the Holy Spirit and my "good idea." The part that was true and of the Lord was that Dianne should use her grandmother's gift for her education. The part that was

103

incorrect was that she should keep all her money in a separate account from her husband.

Soul life causes conflict

The word *soul* is difficult to define because the Bible uses it to indicate the core of us that is spiritually redeemed. Yet it also includes our mind, will, and emotions (see our explanation of the Chart, Chapter 5).

Our soul, according to the Bible, is our inner being where we plan, think, react, and relate to people. This is where we receive and project impressions. It is part of us; it continues to live when our body dies.

The Holy Spirit comes into our spirit and from here flows into our soul life, as we permit His leadership. In this way, the inner being begins to respond to what we receive from God.

For example, as He begins to command and control our actions, we will grow more and more into His likeness. As we read His Word and open various areas of our life to Him, He will increase and we will decrease.

In the realm of wrath, for instance, we will be angry at what displeases God: sin, Satan and anything rearing its head against Him. We will cease flying off the handle when self is afronted.

As God fills our being, as we know His compassion and reality, faith will displace despair. We will not look upon terminal illnesses with panic or desperation. We will know comfort, hope, and healing.

God can take a good trait like human sympathy and convert it. Human sympathy in the area of illness could eventually turn to despair. But if we allow the Holy Spirit freedom to work in all our being, we will know Him as a God who does wonders. And we will be confident and cheerful in the face of seeming calamity. We'll know He's in charge and retain His peace amid turmoil.

The carnal Christian: 1 Corinthians 3:1-3

However, brethren, I could not talk to you as to spiritual [men], but as to nonspiritual (men of the flesh, in whom the carnal nature predominates), as to mere infants [in the new life] in Christ—unable to talk yet!

I fed you with milk, not solid food, for you were not yet strong enough [to be ready for it]; but even yet you are not strong enough [to be ready for it],

For you are still (unspiritual, having the nature) of the flesh—under the control of ordinary impulses. For as long as [there are] envying and jealousy and wrangling and factions among you, are you not unspiritual and of the flesh, behaving yourselves after a human standard and like mere (unchanged) men?

Paul addresses this portion to Spirit-filled believers. They were not ready for the solid food of the Spirit and the Word. They were still drinking the milk. If we indulge our mind, will, and emotions we are "mere (unchanged) men," living in the flesh.

When the soul life operates

The soul incorporates mind (intellect), will (strength of conviction) and emotions (crying, moods, pouting, etc.). When these areas dominate, we conflict with the Holy Spirit.

For example, if my intellect is stubbornly set on a doctrine, I will not hear God's voice. My thinking is crystallized and dogmatic. Therefore, if I am closed to the Spirit on this subject, I will miss His will and slip from His guidance. My mind takes over. And when I propagate this doctrine, using my soul force to persuade others, I bring them into conflict with God, too.

Or suppose my personality is emotional and impulsive. Have you ever been in the grocery store and bought foods without thinking? We can be impetuous in the Spirit, too. Instead of listening to Him, we can direct ourselves and others thoughtlessly and impulsively. For instance, the Lord tells my family to minister to someone tomorrow, but because of impetuousness we go today. In going today, we are disobedient; whatever we say will be adulterated by our soul life.

Children use soul force to influence parents. They learn how to get us to do what they want, and their methods are sometimes ingenious. They know how to wrap parents around their fingers, and they do this by operating in the soul life. If parents and children are communicating on this level, the whole family is serving the soul life, not the Spirit of God.

Soul life goodness vs. God's goodness

We have mentioned before that anything we do apart from God is futile. This was hard for me to accept, because I did many "good," humanitarian acts under the influence of my soul life.

All that we do—even for what seems to be good—without God's anointing only ministers spiritual death, and in God's sight that action is "as filthy rags" (Isaiah 64:6). We only bring life and glorify Him when we achieve under the power of the Holy Spirit.

Out of human sympathy and craving appreciation, I may take food to the home of a poor family. Since I am motivated by my own soulish desires, the life of Jesus is not ministered.

But if He says, "Grace, those people need food," and I take it to them, it will glorify Him and minister His life and health to that family.

Our best is still below God's standard: Isaiah 64:6

For we have all become as one who is unclean [ceremonially, as a leper], and all our righteousness—our best deeds of rightness and justice—are

107

as filthy rags or *a polluted garment. We all fade as a leaf, and our iniquities, like the wind, take us away [far from God's favor, hurrying us to destruction].*

Whom to please?

There may be portions of my thinking, my choices, and my reactions outside the management of the Holy Spirit. If there are, and if I operate in them, I will want to please people. In doing so, I disobey God and am separated from Him. I am acting out of my soul force to please others rather than acting out of faith to please God (Romans 14:23). We have to be confident that whatever results develop from doing what God says are God's problem, not ours. Do not doubt or harbor misgivings about what you do under His power. This sometimes happens when someone else does not like what we have done. We are uneasy because we want to please this unhappy person. Know what God wants and do it. He will take care of people, if we let Him.

Dead emotions hinder responses

In counseling, we have learned that some people's emotions are not even alive to be used by their soul life, let alone by the Holy Spirit.

One way emotions die is through what parents say to children. For instance, when parents spank a son, they tell him, "Boys do not cry." If this is true, and he grows up with this philosophy, then "men do not cry" either. So as a man, he is not able to cry for any reason. His ability to weep has been inhibited.

In the same situation, something else may occur. Parents may say to the child, "Stop crying. I don't want to hear you cry." This trains him to respond passively to pain. A normal child's response to pain is tears. This does not mean the child should be able to cry for an unreasonable length of time. Reconciliation through repentance, forgiveness, prayers for healing when hurt, and other expressions of love will curtail his crying. It will also prevent tears from developing into a tool of soul force to get sympathy or some other kind of attention.

Another thing that deadens emotions is telling youngsters continually, "Behave yourself!" To a child, this means he cannot laugh, giggle, or talk. The only thing he can do is sit with folded hands, hanging onto his emotions. Can you see how difficult it would be for this person, as an adult, to have freedom to worship God in the Spirit? Praying instead for self-control in the Spirit will bring the emotional responses of the body under His control early in life. Later, when the adult worships, he will be free to respond to the Spirit.

Emotions can be bottled up through fear and distrust. We fear what people will do. We fear what they will say. We are threatened by them and distrust them. We are afraid they won't like us, and so we put on a mask to hide our real self.

Rob and I have prayed for many whose emotions were held in a death grip. They had quit feeling, reacting, and having ties with people because of suspicion. In their past they had had too many hurtful experiences with others; so they escaped into a passive attitude.

Many times we annihilate our genuine emotions by covering them up with false ones. When I gave my life to the Lord at nine years of age, I did not want to talk about it. It was sacred to me. After the service, my mother asked me, "What happened?"

"Oh, nothing," I said. And I laughed. I learned from then on to put on a front of laughter to cover up anything real that happened to me.

The emotion of love can grow or die. It can also develop in the wrong way, depending on how a child grows in the family relationship with his parents. We all seek love in our families.

Whether parents are loving the child with human love or with Jesus' love will make a difference in his responses. Love should not depend on what a child does, if he's loved with Jesus' love. In Christ, a child is loved for being himself.

By contrast, human love is conditional: "I will love you when you're good." The child tries desperately to please, but he is bound to fail. He is naturally rebellious and will inevitably make mistakes. Loved with merely human love, he will feel rejected every time he misses the mark.

What if one day I tell my child it is all right to go down the street to play with a friend? Then the next day I tell him he can't. Suppose he goes anyway, because he's confused. Maybe I didn't take the time to explain why he couldn't go. When he returns, I punish him—and without my love. He wants to receive love, and now he doesn't understand what will get him that love.

Let's imagine another situation: a mother wants her daughter to be just like her. To accomplish this, she uses all her will, emotional force, and mind to mold the child. The daughter is put into the place of yielding to her mother's soul force because she wants to be loved and desires to please.

If a child has a sense of rejection early in life, he has a more difficult time accepting love later on. He will also work harder at being loved than the child who matures without parental rejection.

Our emotions can be positive or negative. It depends upon how they are developed. Ideally, they should always be a total fulfilment of what the Spirit within us is saying and feeling. They should be genuine.

Habit patterns cause conflict

Patterns of life are developed from the time we are born. We learn every day how to live in the world, what to do to get along with others and how to get the results we desire. Patterns are endless: money, social, recreation, communication, work, religious, marriage, exercise, learning, etc.

When we come to the Lord—when we are born again and baptized in the Spirit—He gets all our patterns of life. And He gets a mess.

When two people marry from diverse backgrounds, they will do things differently. This is one reason why couples have problems relating to each other. Their patterns conflict.

When Rob and I married we both had our own patterns of life. The one positive thing was that our backgrounds were similar. But even then, the way I had learned to do many things was opposite from the way Rob did things.

Our first conflict came over a corner of the dresser. We both chose to put our things on the same corner. He liked putting his billfold, keys, and loose coins there so in the morning he would not forget to put them back into his pocket. I did the same thing with my rings, watch, and other jewelry.

I remember counseling one family where the man's social area entered into his spiritual life. Every time he shared his Christian faith with someone, he brought him home. And he expected his wife, on short notice, to prepare something for him to eat. His wife did not appreciate having people drop in unexpectedly, so their different patterns caused friction.

Sometimes habits can be compatible but still negative. If two people have the same pattern of judging others, they may enjoy talking together because they enjoy criticizing and condemning others.

Not only do the habits and patterns we bring to marriage cause conflict, but so do the patterns we develop during marriage without the Lord.

Children complicate and expose our patterns, too. How do we want them disciplined? How will we train them? Do we want to live our life over again through them?

One young couple collided bitterly over their first baby. The husband was angry every time the child cried, because no matter what his wife was doing, she ran to comfort the baby. The mother had developed a habit of choosing the child before her husband. The husband got to the point where he hated the baby.

It could be that this mother's pattern was already within her. Maybe she grew up believing a child should be held every time he cried. Or perhaps she only developed this pattern when her baby came into the home.

Patterns can paralyze our life and cause us to be in conflict with the Holy Spirit. When I first married, I started listening to Ma Perkins on the radio. I knew this program was beginning to run my life, because I worked my daily schedule around it.

One morning the Lord said, *"Grace, go to the store when Ma Perkins is on the radio."* I did not obey because I could not live without finding out what happened to her.

Church-going can paralyze us, too. If we attend church because of a duty pattern, then duty controls us. We cannot be free to hear the Holy Spirit if one Lord's Day He asks us to do something else. When churchmanship becomes a tradition, and we are not listening to God, our obligation-to-the-church attitude is, for us, a bondage.

How to change patterns

As we mature in the Lord, He will deal with our patterns, habits, and idiosyncrasies. One way He accomplishes this is by bringing us encounters with others. We learn to bend; our rough edges get sanded.

I had a way of picking up friends and hanging onto them forever. Rob could have a friend, be with him or not, and still be a friend. To me, friendship meant I had to be with them. I wanted to go to all the reunions and homecomings and Rob could have cared less. He loved his friends, but he did not *have* to see them. Our individual social patterns brought us friction.

Rob and I discovered a practical method of handling our individuality so we could begin to function as one. We wanted a compatible marriage and desired to walk with God more than we wanted to hold onto our own way of doing things. So whenever patterns caused problems, we would put ourselves in God's presence and ask Him to cover us with His blood. Then we would ask the Holy Spirit to take from us the particular conflicting pattern, whatever it was, and put in His. This taught us to live under His direction, not under the motivations of our own likes and dislikes.

When Rob and I built our home in San Diego, we both had our own idea of what it should be like. When I studied home economics in college, I designed a house, chose a lot, drew the plans, and built it. The house I designed was a little Cape Cod cottage. Rob's concept of a house was simple, nothing fancy—a house almost empty of anything but the bare essentials.

There is a point where you can agree to disagree. But you also have to be willing to change. It's not valid to state, "That's the way I am. Like it or leave it." Anything can be changed in the Lord. The Cape Cod cottage I constructed as a young collegiate was an idol that had to die. If I'd clung to it, I would have been miserable, selfish, and bitter. Patterns of husband and wife should be pulled;* the Holy Spirit should be allowed to bring in a pattern that is right for both. You cannot say to your spouse, "You live your life, and I'll live mine."

* See "How to Search Patterns," page 145.

In constructing our home, there were times when we got a little emotional in our planning. Most of the time, it was a communication problem. For months I talked about my "modern house" and Rob never knew exactly what I meant. Then one day he discovered my "modern house" had a dishwasher. That, for me, made it modern.

Rob and I prayed over the house we built, and it came out of our two ideas. We both like it. In fifteen years we have not found one thing to regret because we let the Holy Spirit guide us.

Conflicts surface readily when mind, will, and emotions control what we do and say. When we push the Holy Spirit aside in this manner, we are in a direct collision course with God and with others. Expect problems, if this is true in your life. But remember: life is different when the Holy Spirit is in charge.

PRAYER

... to be used after studying Chapters 5 and 6.

Father, we thank You for Your revelation of our natural condition that needs changing by Your Spirit. We can change through the shed blood of Jesus.

Show us how we have been using soul force to get our own way, to get attention, to receive love, and to build relationships. Expose our areas of hurt so we can be healed.

We hang on the cross our old mind, emotions, and will. Crucify them that we might have the mind, emotions, and will of Christ. We ask that these all be converted so we can bring every thought captive to the Lord Jesus Christ. We desire to think Your thoughts and understand Your Word as You want us to live it. We give up our intellect, and ask for Your wisdom and knowledge. We truly want to be able to reason with You.

We put all natural love, affection, and regard for others to death in You; so Your love, affection and regard may come forth through us. We desire to love with Your love, hate with Your perfect hatred, covet what You covet, and have all emotional responses and actions under the control of Your Spirit.

We will to do Your will, O Lord. Take from us with loving force the things in our lives that keep us from the fulfillment of Your will and purpose in our thoughts, words, and deeds. Strengthen us in the inner man to persevere to the end.

We rejoice that You are able to bring this about to Your glory and honor. In Jesus' name. Amen.

7

Charismatic Redemption: Rob's View

Why do Spirit-filled Christians commit adultery?

We knew a Christian whose father told her continually when she was a child, "You are a good girl." As a young woman she commited adultery six times, but without remorse or guilt. She believed she was "good" because her father had said so. No matter what she did, his voice within her kept saying, "You're a good girl."

The principle

God can redeem every area of our life and change us into the likeness of His Son. He knows the answer to every difficulty. And He knows what methods are best in resolving conflicts among His people. The method and the solution may be as unique as the individual.

Solving personality differences

In most cases, sin can be dealt with through repentance. I can ask God and the person I've wronged to forgive me.

Many times God convicts the one that is out of focus, especially if he is teachable, humble, and wants God's will above all else.

Also, if you can agree to disagree on a subject then you are back in unity. But if the disagreement changes how you treat each other, your relationship will be broken, and reconciliation will be in order.

It has helped me when in disagreement to deal first with myself. I quickly pray and hang self on the cross. Jesus then deals with me and I am released to function once again under the Holy Spirit's guidance.

We daily need the blood of Jesus Christ to change, modify, and cleanse all the areas of our lives.

Deliverance may be the only solution

How do Spirit-filled Christians fall into sexual sin?

A young man, whom we considered mature spiritually, was arrested for indecent and homosexual tendencies. In his case, it was not a matter of bringing the cross to bear in ridding his nature of self. He needed deliverance from the power of Satan.

120

How did the enemy get a hold on this young man? We found in counseling that it was through his home environment. His mother tried to make him into a girl, and his father belittled his masculinity constantly.

Do you know Christians who still carry a heavy burden of guilt, even though they've been forgiven by Jesus? Perhaps they need deliverance from a spirit of guilt that binds their thinking and colors their actions. We must deal forcefully with whatever controls us outside of God's Holy Spirit. A deliverance from spiritual bondage may be necessary.*

What if I sin because of pride? Remember my brilliant medical diagnosis? I will have to repent to God for self-glorying. I may also need to ask Grace's forgiveness for being self-righteous. Then I may have to take my self-life and the part of me that wants to boast and hang it on the cross of Jesus. Will I be free after all this? Usually, but not necessarily. I may need to be delivered from a spirit of pride. How did pride imprison me? I did not repent and turn the glory back to the Lord.

* For more on the subject of deliverance, read Don Basham, *Deliver Us From Evil*, (Washington Depot, Conn.: Chosen Books, 1974); Pat Brooks, *Using Your Spiritual Authority*, (Monroeville, Pa.: Whitaker House, 1973); and H. A. Maxwell Whyte, *A Manual on Exorcism*, (Monroeville, Pa.: Whitaker House, 1974).

And each time I gloried, pride took more and more control until the only way to get rid of it was through deliverance.

When I am released, I am free. It is not that I will never be proud again, but in this particular area where Jesus is now enthroned, I would have to deliberately open the door again in order to come under bondage. Once the Holy Spirit takes command and dwells in this area, there is more of His power available to protect me from Satan's onslaughts. Once the spirit of pride is out, the Holy Spirit will help me hold that territory as long as it is my decision to stand with Him.

Problem solving with small groups:
Matthew 18:15-16

If your brother* wrongs you, go and show him his fault, between you and him privately. If he listens to you, you have won back your brother.

But if he does not listen, take along with you one or two others, so that every word may be confirmed and upheld by the testimony of two or three witnesses.

According to these scriptures, when Christians cannot agree, two or three believers are called to listen to the disagreement and give counsel.

---

* The word "brother" means a fellow Christian. This can also apply to a husband/wife relationship, or two sisters or two brothers in the Lord.

If Grace and I could not solve a problem and just kept fighting about it, we could ask mature Christian friends for help. Their job would be to help us communicate and bring us to oneness and loving acceptance of each other.

How would this be accomplished? They would listen to discern where we were out of joint and why we got emotional and upset over the subject in question. Doing this, they would help us pray over the matter to bring our relationship into healing.

My motive for counsel is important, too. It cannot be to prove that "I am right and Grace is wrong." This attitude hinders reconciliation because my motive impedes God's help to us through the Body ministry.

How to listen

Listening involves hearing what is said and penetrating what lies behind the spoken words. Novices, therefore, should not be called in to counsel. They listen with their concepts, ideas, and doctrines, rather than with the Holy Spirit's gift of discernment. When listeners are spiritually mature, the Holy Spirit will make the problem known.

The uninitiated should not counsel because they tend to be too sympathetic. We had a new believer visit one of our counseling sessions. He was just beginning his walk with the Lord. As the group questioned a member seeking spiritual release, the new Christian was hurt by their probing interrogation.

"You were all very unkind to that person," he told me later. But the one counseled was not at all offended and told him so. In fact, the individual was healed and liberated, but the new believer was too spiritually immature to recognize the victory after the searching questions.

How we listen is important. We should be sensitive to the Spirit each time we counsel and not interpret what we hear with past knowledge. Every person is distinct and every individual's problem is different. Face each conflict as unique.

Take your disagreement before the Church: Matthew 18:17

If he pays no attention to them—refusing to listen and obey—tell it to the church; and if he refuses to listen even to the church, let him be to you as a pagan and a tax collector.

What if Grace and I violently disagree and cannot prayerfully solve our problem? What if I am stubborn and locked onto a particular doctrine? Suppose I refuse to listen to anyone else's opinion on the subject? Because of pride, I won't even submit to a small group of believers seeking to bring Grace and me back into unity.

124

What then?

The disagreement is taken before the Church—the Body of believers. My place now is to yield and submit to the Spirit. But what if I don't?

I would be disciplined by the Body, and they would put me for a time out of their fellowship.

The heathen live separated from God:
Ephesians 2:11-13

Therefore remember that at one time you were Gentiles [heathen] in the flesh; called Uncircumcision by those who called themselves Circumcision, [itself a mere mark] in the flesh made by human hands.

Remember that you were at that time separated (living apart) from Christ—excluded from all part in Him; utterly estranged and outlawed from the rights of Israel as a nation, and strangers with no share in the sacred compacts of the [Messianic] promise—with no knowledge of or right in God's agreements, His covenants. And you had no hope—no promise; you were in the world without God.

But now in Christ Jesus, you who once were [so] far away, through (by, in) the blood of Christ have been brought near.

If I refuse to listen to the Church's counsel, I am to be treated as a heathen because I am rebellious.

The heathen's way of life is futile:
Ephesians 4:17, 18

So this I say and solemnly testify in [the name of] the Lord [as in His Presence,] that you must no longer live as the heathen (the Gentiles) do in their perverseness—in the folly, vanity and emptiness of their souls and the futility—of their minds.

Their moral understanding is darkened and their reasoning is beclouded. [They are] alienated (estranged, self-banished) from the life of God—with no share in it. [This is] because of the ignorance—the want of knowledge and perception, the willful blindness—that is deep-seated in them, due to their hardness of heart (to the insensitiveness of their moral nature).

Here is a portrait of a proud heathen. I, too, could be like him. I could exalt my intellectualism, my arguments, and my art of persuasion and be held prisoner by my own doctrinal position. Therefore, my understanding would be darkened and I could not listen to counsel. Nor could I receive truth from God's people. In this state I would be like a heathen.

The believer outside the Church's fellowship:
1 Timothy 1:19, 20

Keeping fast hold on faith [that leaning of the entire human personality on God in absolute trust
126

and confidence] and a good (clear) conscience. By rejecting and thrusting from them [their conscience,] some individuals have made shipwreck of their faith.

Among them are Hymenaeus and Alexander, whom I have delivered to Satan in order that they may be disciplined [by punishment and learn] not to blaspheme.

By not submitting to the Church's counsel, I ignore their faith and shipwreck mine. I put myself out of fellowship and am delivered over to Satan for testing and trial.

Peter was sifted like grain: Luke 22:31, 32

Simon, Simon (Peter), listen! Satan has asked excessively that (all of) you be given up to him—out of the power and keeping of God—that he might sift (all of) you like grain,

But I have prayed especially for you [Peter] that your [own] faith may not fail; and when you yourself have turned again, strengthen and establish your brethren.

The Lord permitted Satan to test Job: Job 1:6-12

Now there was a day when the sons [the angels] of God came to present themselves before the Lord, so Satan—the adversary and accuser—also came among them.

And the Lord said to Satan, From where did you come? Then Satan answered the Lord, From going to and fro on the earth, and from walking up and down on it.

And the Lord said to Satan, Have you considered My servant Job, that there is none like him on the earth, a blameless and upright man, one who (reverently) fears God and abstains from and shuns evil [because it is wrong]?

Then Satan answered the Lord, Does Job (reverently) fear God for nothing?

Have You not put a hedge about him and his house and all that he has, on every side? You have conferred prosperity and happiness upon him in the work of his hands, and his possessions have increased in the land.

But put forth Your hand now, and touch all that he has, and he will curse You to Your face.

And the Lord said to Satan—the adversary and the accuser—Behold, all that he has is in your power; only upon himself put not forth your hand. So Satan went forth from the presence of the Lord.

In this case, Job was righteous but God allowed him to endure trial.

Israel sifted: Amos 9:9

For, lo, I will command, and I will sift the house of Israel among all nations and cause it to move to and fro, like as grain is sifted in a sieve, yet shall not the least kernel fall upon the earth and be lost [from My sight].

The Church's responsibility to the brother out of fellowship

When the Church puts me out of fellowship, they have a responsibility. They must pray that I will turn again to the Lord and return to my place in His Body. They must pray for me to submit and repent to God and man.

Maybe I have a self problem in being submissive and returning to the fellowship. I say, "I do not want to. I will not." It's only through their intercession that my self will come to the place of saying, "I will."

If this were true, the group might not only be dealing with my self-life, but with many other factors. Perhaps I had early life experiences of being trapped by others, manipulated by people. Maybe I am afraid of being caught, or fearful of being put on the spot. This would make it even harder for me to submit to the Body of believers.

Or maybe I am not submissive because I have put my trust in someone who disappointed me. This traumatic experience keeps me from trusting others, including the Body of believers and even my own wife.

When you are praying for a Christian brother living in sin, keep these things in mind. Be sensitive to the Spirit and pray the prayers He leads you to pray. Remember, too, all the teachings of love and forgiveness (Matthew 18:21, 22). Don't cast anyone from your fellowship because

129

he makes a mistake. We all do that. Put him out for a while only if he comes to the place where he is not repentant or refuses to be reconciled.

Handling conflicts caused by pseudo-prophets

Previously, we mentioned that one way we sin is by neglecting to test the prophets and their message.

Prophecy is a supernatural gift which can include aspects of advice, counsel, teaching, preaching, prediction, something foretold, communication and the interpretation of the divine will and purpose.

God's message holds up under examination:
1 Corinthians 2:15, 16

But the spiritual man tries all things—[that is] he examines, investigates, inquires into, questions, and discerns all things; yet is himself to be put on trial and judged by no one.—He can read the meaning of everything, but no one can properly discern or appraise or get an insight into him.

For who has known or understood the mind (the counsels and purposes) of the Lord so as to guide and instruct [Him] and give Him knowledge? But we have the mind of Christ, the Messiah, and do hold the thoughts (feelings and purposes) of His heart.

We cannot question the Holy Spirit's guidance for another. But we can certainly question another person's guidance for us.

A few years ago Grace received two letters. The messages, from two groups separated by hundreds of miles, were similar. Both said: "God told us you were to speak to us Sunday at 10 o'clock."

Could they both be God's will? Hardly.

We have found people quoting God, but this does not mean God said what they said. We tested this guidance for Grace by prayer, asking God's confirmation or rejection. He gave us the right answer.

Let's consider Peter again. Remember his revelation from God? "Thou art the Christ, the Son of the Living God," he said to Jesus. But moments later, Christ rebuked Satan in his counsel. See how quickly we can slip into the soul life even in the realm of prophecy?

Let's assume that in a believers' meeting a young man receives this prophetic message: "The Lord says you are to go to Bali Bali as a missionary."

If he accepts this utterance and submits to it, without a confirmation from God, he will be in bondage. Perhaps God is leading him to be a chemist. By believing the prophet, he will fight God's truth for his life.

Testing the prophet's message:
Deuteronomy 18:20-22

But the prophet who presumes to speak a word in My name which I have not commanded him to

131

speak, or who speaks in the name of other gods, that same prophet shall die.

And if you say in your [mind and] heart, How shall we know which words the Lord has not spoken?

When a prophet speaks in the name of the Lord, if the word does not come to pass or prove true, that is a word which the Lord has not spoken; the prophet has spoken it presumptuously; you shall not be afraid of him.

Time tests the prophet's message. Does it come to pass? If you receive a message through another Christian, hold it loosely. Yield to the Spirit so you can move in His direction.

The young man called to Bali Bali as a missionary should examine that call. As he proceeds in his walk with the Lord and receives an education, he could see how God guided. To the mission field or to the field of chemistry?

Obedience is a vital ingredient. When it comes down to basics, no one can be the voice of God for another. Hearing the Lord speak is each believers' responsibility. Others may confirm His word to us, but they cannot be His channel of communication for us. Prove all things and hold fast to that which is good (1 Thessalonians 5:21).

8

Charismatic Redemption: Grace's View

The reason we react from the soul life is because it is not yet changed. But it can be redeemed in Jesus.

Our soul force must come under the leadership of the Holy Spirit so He controls our mind, will, and emotions rather than self or Satan. Then our reactions will be Christ-like.

We have to work with God for this change. We have to allow Him to change our natural man into the likeness of Jesus.

First, allow the Holy Spirit to fill your spirit. Then from there, permit Him to take complete control of your soul and body.

This is only possible because Jesus died on the cross to redeem us. Without Him, we would continue to operate in the soul life, and our mind, will, and emotions would take over and control the spirit life.

The principle

To receive God's answer, we must repent. Then He can show us the problem, how to receive His redemption, and how to extend His deliverance into the lives of those with whom we are in conflict.

Conflicts resolved in God's presence:
2 Kings 19:14-16

Hezekiah received the letter from the hand of the messengers, and read it. And he went up into the house of the Lord, and spread it before the Lord.

And Hezekiah prayed: O Lord the God of Israel, Who [in symbol] are enthroned above the cherubim [of the ark in the temple], You are the God, You alone, of all the kingdoms of the earth; You have made the heavens and the earth.

Lord, bow down Your ear and hear; Lord, open Your eyes and see; hear the words of Sennacherib, which he has sent to mock, reproach, insult and defy the living God.

In my conflict with Rob and Dianne (Chapter 6), I asked the Lord to show me my problem. I told Him honestly how I felt about the whole thing. I explained to Him my lack of understanding why I was wrong. And I repeated what my family thought about the situation. He showed me that half-truths were operating, and that that was my basic problem. When He revealed this, I went

134

at once to Rob and Dianne and asked them to forgive me. The Lord allowed this confrontation so my half-truths could be judged, looked at closely, and changed.

If you have a conflict, be honest and open before the Lord. Tell Him about it. Lay the details before Him. He has a solution for you. In fact, God allows us to have problems. Not that it pleases Him if we are depressed by them. Nor is He pleased when we seek answers in our own mind. He wants us to come to Him, voice our moans and groans, and then let Him do something about the difficulty.

Do not get the idea, either, that when you lay your case before Him everyone else will change. You may be the one to change. But He will look at the problem with you and show you where you need to repent, and what areas need to be changed through the blood of Jesus. If you need to ask anyone's forgiveness, He will let you know. He will reveal where you are right, too. And then He will show you what you can expect Him to do.

Soul force can be redeemed

In 1 Corinthians 5:1-13, Paul tells the Church in Corinth that the person is still living in the soul areas and wants to continue living there. Because of this, he counsels, "Put him out and let him live his own way until he comes to the end of himself." When he came to the end of his own way, the prodigal repented.

If someone insists on living in his soul life, God allows it until he comes to the end of his own plans. The one alienated from the Lord must willingly turn to Him, repent and allow God's Spirit to transform him. Many times repentance involves not only God, but others who were hurt by a person's soul force. Repentance and forgiveness heal relationships.

Keep praying for a person willing to repent, even if he uses soul force again and again. We have to forgive "seventy times seven." Through prayer, that unredeemed area will finally be taken over by the Spirit.

"Be perfect as your heavenly Father is perfect" (Matthew 5:48) is a possibility for all believers. Scriptural perfection is maturity and should be every Christian's goal.

When our soul life has been touched by the Holy Spirit and changed by the blood of Christ, self will not control our mind, will, or emotions. God can now use them. We are not serving self any more. We serve God.

Soul force at work

When God showed me that what I had done in my soul life was unacceptable to Him, I was devastated. I'd done a lot of good deeds. But I gave these good things to the Spirit of God and put them to death on the cross. He delivered me from all my human goodness and freed me to act as He led.

Being a good person is not enough to please God. He requires holiness (1 Peter 1:16). He requires that our goodness be under the Spirit's control so that whatever worthy deed we do will be because He first said, "Do it."

I did much to please and help people. Not only was my self life active, but a spirit of pleasing others dictated orders. When I asked God to govern that area of my life, I had to reckon dead in Jesus the self that pleased people and wanted to help them. Then the binding force within me of pleasing others was cast out in the name of Jesus for my deliverance.

With this cleansing, I came to a place where I could judge what people asked of me. Does their request come from the Spirit? If it came from soul force, I asked God if I should comply. I was very joyful the day I was free to ask God and not have to say "yes" to people because of my own soul force's desire to please.

Only God knows if we should cooperate when we are solicited to do something. Listen with the Spirit to every demand upon your life. We have more discernment and awareness when our soul area is cleansed. But if it is not under the Spirit's authority, others can work on us to the point that we cannot resist. We will be driven by others and not led by the Spirit.

If children get everything they want through soul force, rather than yielding to the Spirit for what God wants, the self will grow stronger and the soul will dominate the spirit.

We have been taught to allow children to express themselves any way they wish, but this self-expression has to come under the authority of the Lord.

Teach your children how to listen to God. Teach them that what they want is not always what God wants for them. We can only teach this if we ourselves are changed and know how to express ourselves under the rule of the Holy Spirit.

Redemption for conflicts caused by patterns

Jesus brings our natural patterns of life into confrontation with others. He does this so our patterns can be redeemed by Him and exchanged for His patterns. It is important to realize this. If we are willing for God to change us, it is less difficult for Him to deal with us.

Rob and I desired above everything else to walk in the Holy Spirit and to do God's will. With this as our cornerstone, we learned how to evaluate our different patterns and see where we were in opposition. We learned to be transparent with each other and, having this attitude, God's solution to our contentions came quickly.

138

If we had obstinately insisted on our own way and refused to bend, solving even simple problems would have been impossible. We would have battled daily over little things like who gets the corner of the dresser.

All conflicts caused by clashing patterns can be solved. But we must yield to God, asking Him to put our patterns under the blood of Jesus and under the Spirit's authority. Maybe we'll have to change these patterns completely. And we can, through the power of the Holy Spirit.

If we have hurt our spouse, children, or friends because of our patterns, we need to ask forgiveness. This heals relationships.

Many people do not want to give up old ways of doing things. But Jesus' perfect patterns will always be better, no matter how good previous patterns were in the natural.

When a person is required by God to do something, it may involve another individual. Rob was very active in Kiwanis Club when the Lord told him to give it up. The Holy Spirit had other things for him to do. Resigning was a difficult decision for Rob, because he was vice-president that year and in line for the presidency.

And when he resigned, I too had to deal with my club pattern. I couldn't belong to the ladies' group connected with Kiwanis unless Rob was a club member.

God modified and changed many of our patterns. I was entrenched in my social patterns concerning friends. I had to put my friends on God's altar, so I could be happy to see them only as He indicated. Many times I was possessed by a yearning to be with old friends. Even when I fellowshipped with others and knew I was in the center of God's plan for the moment, I found myself wishing I were with my old friends instead. I had to learn to love friends and be separated from them.

It is not that the Lord was cutting people out of my life just to cut them out. He wanted them in their rightful place so I could conform to His plans.

Jesus fits families together

The love fellowship founded on Jesus makes it possible for sin to manifest and half-truths and untruths to surface. Love exposes soul force and reveals pattern differences. In all conflicts the Lord is the problem solver. And He is creating in our homes and in our lives freedom for His Holy Spirit to flow unhindered without the obstacles of self, traditions, and patterns.

PRAYER

... to be used at conclusion of studying Chapters 7 and 8.

Father, by Your Spirit reveal to us the soul area still operating in our lives. If our emotions are dead, we pray that You bring them to life by Your Spirit.

Lord, where we have had our emotions warped so they are now being used the wrong way, we ask You to bring them forth by the power of the Holy Spirit. Make our reactions genuine, reflecting our true person.

Lord, we pray that You will heal all the wounds in our memory regarding our emotions. Free our tears and laughter to be useful to You at the proper time. Heal our broken hearts. Restore us to wholeness in our will, mind, and emotions.

Lord, we command any spirit of anger or jealousy that has come in because it was used by our soul to be gone in the name of Jesus.

Lord, convert all of our emotions and bring them under the power of the Holy Spirit. Reveal to us all our dead emotions, so we can pray them into new life under the Spirit's direction.

We command the fear of being fearful to go in

the name of Jesus, and the fear of being exposed and fear of being genuine to be cast out.

Lord, we submit our wills to You that only Your will can be done, not the will of soul force. Free our wills to choose You and Your holy plan for us.

Teach us how to yield to Your Spirit at all times. We want Your will above our own. Teach us, Lord, how to walk by the Spirit and not by the flesh. Teach us how to be totally related to You, to be genuine and whole, and to glorify and honor You in all things.

We thank You and praise You for Jesus, the perfect pattern of how to live life and how to meet its problems. We ask You to reveal those things that You want dealt with by Your Spirit, those patterns of life, and those half-truths that we have grown to believe are right and true and good, but that in reality are not of You.

We pray that by Your Spirit You will minister life to us in the areas that have need. We yield up our money patterns, our attitudes towards strangers at the door, people coming into our home—we give You what is recreation in our home, what is correct behavior, social graces that we have accepted to be proper. We give You all that we are and ask that You, Jesus, will give us Your social pattern. We give to You all our patterns of recreation. We ask You to come and teach us how to enjoy life by Your Spirit through fun at various activities and relationships with people.

142

Lord, we yield up the patterns of raising and disciplining our children and relating to them. If there are any disagreements in us where our children are concerned, we yield these to You. Let Your love take the place of disagreement.

Lord, we ask You to search us and find out what is really true about the things that have happened in our lives. Show each of us the lies within us, the things we have buried so we don't have to look at them. Father, by Your Spirit search out truth. Take all our pretense and make us real. Bring forth the true person we were meant to be, standing firmly in the place You have for us to fill.

Father, lead and guide us by Your Spirit into the wholeness of life You have planned. In the name of Jesus. Amen.

How to Search Patterns

Searching patterns is one way of dealing with them. Some can be prayed about and put under the Spirit's control. Others can be pulled and Jesus' pattern put in its place. But some need to be searched for further and deeper cleansing.

As an illustration of how to search patterns, let's look at just one: the play pattern.

For example:

Write down the names of games you played from the time you were little until now. Under each one write your fears, your feelings, and the incidents that happened while playing these games.

What was the influence of the world and the flesh in playing the games? Was there any Satanic influence?

If you did not play games, what did you do in your spare time and why?

Were you disobedient during play time?

What was your family participation in games, picnics, vacations, trips, fun, home, free time, concerts, circus, fairs, races, competitive sports?

What was your participation with your peer group and other people?

What were the things you did in your play time that you were not free to tell your parents?

What areas need repentance? What memories bring guilt?

When the Lord leads you to search any pattern, be honest in His Presence. After searching, ask His forgiveness and pray for healing and deliverance as the Spirit leads. Then pull the pattern and ask for Jesus' perfect pattern in its place. This brings restoration. If you need to change in your personal reactions, you will, because now you are governed by the Holy Spirit in that area.

The only genuine life we have is when every pattern has been carefully looked at with Him and He is put in charge. Transforming His people is something God does gradually. We would be in continual turmoil if God went down into our subconscious mind and pulled up every pattern. We cannot change all at once. Growing into His likeness is a lifetime process.

But remember, it is always too soon to give up.

Don't be impatient if you are slow to mature. If you still have friction, that is good. God permits conflicts so you can look at them and change, if necessary.

As you deal with the various things God reveals, He will transfer you from the realm of the soul life. And you will begin to operate under His instructions.

You must come to Him with an honest heart and look at all areas where patterns have developed. Do not fear making mistakes. Do not fear exposure, or failure.

Sometimes people think they are being candid. Actually, they have lied so often to themselves to cover up, they believe the lie is true.

A minister asked a policeman how fast he could drive above the speed limit without getting a ticket. He convinced himself it wasn't sin to exceed the limit, because he wouldn't be caught.

Another Spirit-filled believer indulged in adultery because, he said, "I am teaching this girl how to love." In counseling, we helped him intellectually to see he was lying to himself, and he repented and was delivered.

Be sure to tell the whole story. One woman who came for counseling only told part of her difficulty, and therefore received only partial healing. She was afraid we would think she was a "horrible person." Two years later she returned to tell the entire story. That time she was completely restored.

Do not be afraid of truth. It will set you free.

Searching Questions

... to be used at conclusion of studying Chapters 1 and 2.

1. Did you choose your spouse or did God? Are you happy with the choice? If not, why? Do you ever think of others you might have married? If so, cleanse them from your heart. Do you feel "chosen"? Do you feel content, trapped, resigned, resentful?

2. If you are a wife, how do you feel about being a woman? Do you ever wish you were a man?

3. If you are a husband, how do you feel about being a man? Do you ever wish you were a woman?

4. If you are a husband, what does being the head of your home as Christ is the head of the Church mean to you? Does it mean being supreme ruler or joint heir with your wife?

5. What does the word submission mean to you? To whom do you submit?

6. Are you afraid of your spouse? Does he or she represent someone else to you?

7. Are you totally dependent on one another? Or are you independent?

8. If you are a wife, who chose your husband's work?

9. Are there changes you would make in your life if you could?

10. Do you feel you have "missed it" in any way?

11. Do you feel you are in God's perfect will? If not, why?

12. Do you like your spouse? Do you choose him or her for a companion? Do you anticipate time together? Do you dread encounters? Do you watch what you say or do around each other?

13. Do you look forward to a long life together? Do you dread retirement? Do you have plans?

14. Can you recognize when Satan is using your spouse? Can you recognize when Jesus is controlling your spouse's actions? Can you submit to the Christ in your spouse and resist Satan's attacks?

15. Do you have any fears, guilts, dreads; any memories of hurtful experiences with your spouse?

Searching Questions

... to be used at conclusion of studying Chapters 3 and 4.

1. Are you in bondage to anyone? If so, why? Is it because of money? Is it because of other obligations?

2. Do you hold anyone in bondage? Do you demand allegiance from anyone?

3. Have you really left home and parents? Are you cleaving only to your spouse?

4. Do you use your children against your spouse?

5. Have you released your children? Where haven't you?

6. Do you have a relationship that is meaningful with all members of your family? If not, what do you think hinders the relationship? What makes relationships meaningful?

7. Is there favoritism in your family?

8. Do you feel valuable and worthwhile in your family?

9. Do you make your children feel meaningful?

10. Are you in bondage to family traditions? Which ones? Why?

11. What are the lies Satan has told you about breaking bondages? Has he suggested it is not loving? Has he said it will hurt others and that Christians do not hurt people? Has he said you should do everything your parents ask? Has he told you parents are above spouse when it comes to desires?

12. What access do your neighbors have to your home?

13. What are you teaching your children about neighbors, relatives, friends? Do you tell them one thing and live another? Do you talk about people in your home? What tone does your conversation take? What do your children learn from the way you converse?

14. Where are you uncomfortable with neighbors or friends?

15. Are you able to repent to neighbors or friends? Are you able to forgive them?

16. Are you in bondage to neighbors or friends?

17. Are you free to hear God's voice in the neighbor or family situation? Are you free to do what God says? Do you really desire to be free?

18. Do you allow neighbors or relatives to borrow whenever they wish? Are you obligated to neighbors or relatives in any way? Do you borrow freely from your friends, relatives, and neighbors? Can you say no to neighbors or friends?

19. Are you active in coffee clutches? What does it mean to you?

20. Do neighbors or friends use you and your possessions?

21. Who are your children's playmates? Do they encourage your children to rebel or obey?

22. Do you let your children's friends come to your home and spend the night? If not, why?

23. Do you buy your children toys because other children in the neighborhood have them?

24. Do you allow your children to mess up the yard with toys or games? Or do you send them to the neighbors' house to play?

25. Do you allow your children to go to neighbors' homes at meal time? Do you allow your neighbors' children to come to your home at meal time? Do you feed your neighbors' children? Are you free to send them home? If not, why?

26. Are you in control of neighbor situations or are your neighbors?

27. Are you a "good" neighbor? Are you a "good" relative? Do you have to do everything everyone wants?

28. Can you handle situations when neighbors' pets bark, dig up your flowers, or mess on your yard? Do you pray through with God whatever you do? Can you speak lovingly with your neighbor?

29. Are you jealous of your neighbors and friends? Do you try to keep up with the Joneses?

30. Are you resentful of your neighbor if he mows his lawn with his power lawnmower Sunday morning at 6 A.M.?

31. Do you have any memories that need to be healed concerning neighbors, friends, or relatives.

32. Do you have any guilts, fears, or resentments that need to be cleansed in the area of neighbor/friend/relative relationships?

Searching Questions

... to be used at conclusion of studying Chapters 5 and 6.

1. What forms of soul force do you use to get your own way? Do you use tears, anger, sweetness, favors, strong words, silent treatment, pouting, positive statements like "I'm right," commands, superstitions, flat statements, a deadpan face, pretend innocence, empty reasoning, changing the subject, diverting attention, covering up by pretending it didn't happen? Do you put guilt on the other person: "You never let me do anything"? Or, "So and so gets to"? Do you say, "Wouldn't you like to?" thereby giving an option with no choice? Do you plead sympathy, act woebegone, get sick, show fatigue? Are you persistent, stubborn, jealous, envious? Do you use cutting words, a sense of humor? Do you lie, or put up a false front?

2. Do you need to repent of any sin? Do you need to repent *to* anyone because of a conflict caused by your sin?

3. Where are your half-truths? Are you willing for God to reveal them and deal with them? Where are you still standing on ideas, instead of on Jesus and His truth?

4. Where have you trusted in prophecy that brought friction and confusion? Has that prophetic message been prayed off?

Searching Questions

... to be used at conclusion of studying Chapters 7 and 8.

1. How do you settle differences? Are they resolved by the Holy Spirit, or by self? Do you quit or try to escape the problem?

2. Are you free to be the one to change?

3. Do you avoid talking about any areas of life? Do you agree on most things?

4. Are you free to fight, or do you want peace at any price?

5. Where do you cop out in confronting a problem?

6. What causes the most conflicts in your family?

7. Can your family make an agreement all members can keep?

8. Are you free to repent to your spouse and children, admitting you were wrong? If not, why? Are you too proud, self-righteous? Do you not want to give others the satisfaction of being right? Do you have to be right?

9. Do you desire your family redeemed? Are you willing to pay what it might cost?

Suggested Inspirational
Paperback Books

THE ACTS OF THE GREEN APPLES
by Jean Stone Willians $1.45

Once upon a time, the Willianses were quiet, respectable suburbanites. The story of how they got to Hong Kong is the heart-warming, miracle-studded and frankly hilarious account of *The Acts of the Green Apples*.

CLIMB MOUNT MORIAH
by Pat Brooks $1.25

A fascinating study of people who have passed through life's darkest moments, facing prospects of broken marriage and adultery, financial ruin and disgrace. They learned how to tap vast reservoirs of spiritual power and come through to victory——and so can you!

FACE UP WITH A MIRACLE
by Don Basham $1.25

This is a fascinating book about God the Holy Spirit bringing a new dimension into the lives of twentieth-century Christians. It is filled with experiences that testify to a God of miracles being unleashed in our lives right now.

FAITH UNDER FIRE
by Chris Panos   95¢

Learn the secrets of fiery faith, as Chris Panos shares with you the insights that have enabled him to heal the sick, win thousands of souls to Christ, and smuggle Bibles into Iron and Bamboo Curtain countries at the risk of his life.

GILLIES' GUIDE TO HOME PRAYER MEETINGS
by George and Harriet Gillies $1.25

He is a retired Wall Street executive. She is his wife. Together, they wrote *A Scriptural Outline of the Baptism in the Holy Spirit*. Now the Gillies bring us this practical, step-by-step handbook dealing with the problems and procedures involved in setting up the kind of home fellowship that will bless the lives of all attending.

HOW GREAT I WAS!
by Doug Foley $1.25

Doug Foley was a young, ambitious engineer who woke up one morning to find all his dreams shattered by the words of a neurologist who told him, "You've got disseminated sclerosis." *How Great I Was* is the gripping true story of the miracles that brought Doug Foley back to health in spirit, mind, and body.

HE SPOKE AND I WAS STRENGTHENED
by Dick Mills $1.25

An easy-to-read devotional of 52 prophetic scripturally-based messages directed to the businessman, the perfectionist, the bereaved, the lonely, the ambitious and many more.

IF I CAN, YOU CAN
by Betty Lee Esses $2.25

The wife of charismatic teacher Michael Esses tells how Jesus saved her husband and her marriage and shares what He's been teaching the Esses ever since. For Betty, these were hard-won spiritual insights. For you, they can come easy; all you have to do is read this book.

IF YOU SEE LENNIE
by Char Potterbaum $1.45

Char Potterbaum was so full of pills her husband claimed she rattled when she turned over in bed. Learn why she doesn't need pills anymore—and how she exchanged her depression for joy—in a book that combines everyday, homespun humor with true spiritual wisdom.

KICKED OUT OF THE KINGDOM
by Charles Trombley $1.25

It all began with a totally unexpected *miracle*—healing of his baby daughter's clubbed feet. Trombley's Jehovah's Witness friends said, "The devil did it!" But Trombley asked, "Would the devil do anything as beautiful as this?" From beginning to end, this is the story of God's sovereign move in the life of a man who really wanted to know the truth.

LET GO!
by Fenelon   95¢

Jesus promised a life full of joy and peace. Why then are so many Christians struggling to attain the qualities that Christ said belonged to the child of God? Fenelon speaks firmly—but lovingly—to those whose lives have been an uphill battle. Don't miss this one.

A MANUAL ON EXORCISM
by H. A. Maxwell Whyte $1.25

The Exorcist posed the question; this book has the answers. Are there really such things as demons? How can you know if you have one? Can anybody cast out demons? These and many more troublesome questions are clearly answered in this helpful book.

THE NEW WINE IS BETTER
by Robert Thom $1.45

Anyone with problems (and who hasn't got problems?) needs to read this story of one man who saw the invisible, believed the incredible, and received the impossible. A lively and often amusing account of Robert Thom's downward trek from a 12 bedroom mansion in South Africa to the hopeless world of an alcoholic on the verge of suicide—and the whole new world of faith and power Robert Thom discovered after Mrs. Webster came knocking on his door.

PLEASE MAKE ME CRY
by Cookie Rodriguez
$1.45

The first female dope addict to "kick the habit" in Dave Wilkerson's ministry, Cookie was so hard people said even death didn't want her. Told the way it really happened, this is the true story of how Cookie found Someone she wanted even more than heroin.

_____WHEREVER PAPERBACKS ARE SOLD OR USE THIS COUPON_____

Whitaker House
504 LAUREL DRIVE, MONROEVILLE, PA 15146

SEND INSPIRATIONAL BOOKS LISTED BELOW

Title	Price	☐ Send Complete Catalog
_____	_____	
_____	_____	
_____	_____	
_____	_____	
_____	_____	
_____	_____	
_____	_____	
_____	_____	

NAME_____

STREET_____

CITY_____ STATE_____ ZIP_____